I0067842

The Sales Momentum Mindset

The Sales Momentum Mindset

Igniting and Sustaining Sales Force Motivation

Gregory S. Chambers

BEP

BUSINESS EXPERT PRESS

Leader in applied, concise business books

The Sales Momentum Mindset: Igniting and Sustaining Sales Force Motivation

Copyright © Business Expert Press, LLC, 2024

Cover design and illustrations by Damir Kundalic

Interior design by Exeter Premedia Services Private Ltd., Chennai, India

All rights reserved. No part of this publication may be reproduced, stored in a retrieval system, or transmitted in any form or by any means—electronic, mechanical, photocopy, recording, or any other except for brief quotations, not to exceed 400 words, without the prior permission of the publisher.

First published in 2023 by
Business Expert Press, LLC
222 East 46th Street, New York, NY 10017
www.businessexpertpress.com

ISBN-13: 978-1-63742-528-2 (paperback)
ISBN-13: 978-1-63742-529-9 (e-book)

Business Expert Press Selling and Sales Force Management Collection

First edition: 2023

10 9 8 7 6 5 4 3 2 1

To my lovely bride, our beautiful children, family, friends, and clients. Plus, Wilson the Amazing Border Collie (nothing happens around here without his express approval).

Description

Unleash your sales potential with *The Sales Momentum Mindset*. This transformative guide is the key to unlocking sustainable sales force motivation by doing something radical: ignoring motivation. Crafted for sales professionals and managers alike, it offers a fresh perspective on sales performance, designed to ignite production and guide teams toward unprecedented growth.

Discover the power that comes from focusing on momentum instead of motivation, understand its impact on sales culture, and learn how to convert it into significant, lasting results. Gain insights into a new language and framework around momentum, presented in a down-to-earth narrative that will resonate with every level of sales experience.

Authored by a seasoned sales veteran, the book's authentic stories and enlightening visuals reveal an innovative approach to sales performance management. Find what's achievable when you step away from obsolete motivational approaches, and instead cultivate a *momentum mindset*.

No matter what you sell or your level of experience, *The Sales Momentum Mindset* is set to revolutionize your perception of sales and sales force management. Step into a new era of sales success. **This is your manual for momentum-based sales transformation.**

Regular updates and more opportunities to learn at chamberspivot.com

Keywords

sales leadership skills; sales motivation tips; sales strategy and planning; sales performance management; developing sales team; storytelling in sales; best books for sales managers; sales inspiration; sales motivational speakers; tools for sales managers; sales management techniques; sales team motivation activities; salesforce well-being; sales motivation; sales mindset; daily sales motivation; emotional intelligence in sales; motivational message for sales team; sales coaching techniques; change management in sales; driving sales performance; effective sales training methods;

incentives for sales reps; methods of sales control; motivational books for salespeople; sales management and leadership; sales management theory; sales productivity tips; training methods for sales manager

Contents

Acknowledgments

A special thank you to everyone I've worked with or asked for stories from: Laura, Abby, David, Matt, and Paige. Jenny, Kirk, Bill and Michelle T, my parents and in-laws, UFG, Dr. Janie, Bert and Suzie, Esteban, Julia, RobJ, LisaJ, Jeff, Cathy, Dan and Karen, Katie G, G-Money, Lisa, Vince, Drewstafa, Debbie, Dean from Down Under, Dillon, Tara, Vikram, Brad, TJ O, Brett, Dan Rehal, Mr. Carl, Bill Ryan, Spence, Tommy G, my bro-from-another-mother Bill M, the other Bill M, Craig, cousin Kevin, Joanie, Meghan, Mike, the hundreds of subscribers of my weekly *Right FIT Newsletter*, and countless others. (Most of whom don't know I am sitting there, watching and listening, like some sales-obsessed Elf on the Shelf!)

I am grateful to the community of Alan Weiss, PhD, the Society for the Advancement of Consulting, and Mahan Khalsa, who inspire me by serving their clients with equal parts IQ and EQ. Thank you all.

Introduction

Motivation dominates sales and selling cultures. A quick search in my inbox for the word "motivation" delivers hundreds of results. I've been in sales and sales management my entire career and this inbox goes back to the late 2000s, so it's a decent barometer. On the other hand, when I search for the word "momentum," there are fewer instances. Most of them are e-mails or newsletters or commentary from me. This makes sense, because I've been obsessed with the idea that we in the sales profession should be spending less time and effort working on motivating our salespeople and more time thinking about building and maintaining our salespeople's momentum (see Figure I.1).

When talking about this concept with executives and sales leaders, we struggle trying to define sales momentum. However, we almost instinctively know to respect momentum when we see it. When a top seller is "on a roll" we get out of their way and make an extra effort to help them continue their "hot streak," but we don't talk about it. Much like a baseball pitcher who is working on a No Hitter, we don't dare mention the word around someone on a roll for fear of scaring the momentum away. Instead, we put in a little extra effort to keep the No Hitter going. We don't ruffle their feathers; we don't ask too many questions. We clear the path ahead.

Figure I.1 Momentum

It's a human response. We've been socialized for it. As a matter of fact, when we see someone on a roll we don't think about their motivation because it's there, inside them. Just look! How else could they get those results?

On the other hand, if we see a salesperson struggling, the first thing we do is look inside for motivation. In our brain it sounds like, "Why are they not hitting quota? What's going on in that head of theirs? They must not care. Let's motivate them."

Another way of saying this is, we assume good results come from internal motivation, so bad results must mean a lack of motivation. In either case, struggling or on a roll, our instinct is to ignore the role of friction or environmental factors in producing results.

Spoiler alert: Friction points and environmental factors are what we're going to focus on in this book. Momentum needs a spark from motivation to get going, but in order to build up to anything resembling a "hot streak," friction and environmental factors need to be removed or minimized.

I Learned This in Grade School

My earliest experience with momentum, motivation, and friction and their effect on sales results came in grade school. I didn't comprehend it at the time, but this story illustrates the difference between motivation and action, and why I think we will do more for sales when we focus on momentum, removing obstacles and friction, rather than focusing on motivation.

Picture a little grade school in Denver, Colorado. We're a parochial school with maybe 400 students. In the first through third grade, we get exposed to the school fund raiser, selling raffle tickets. It's an annual event that provides the school with much-needed income for teacher salaries and operations. The annual festival culminates in a raffle drawing for a substantial cash prize. While every family is encouraged to buy tickets, the fourth- through eighth-grade students are encouraged to sell them to the public. My classrooms in first through third grade are on the same floor as the principal's office. Next to the principal's office there is a trophy case and every year the trophies were removed and the raffle ticket sales prizes went in. These are things every child of the 1970s wants. Sell the minimum number of tickets, get something lame, like a school pendant. Sell a lot more than the minimum and you can win an amazing prize, like a video game system, which at the time is new and too pricey for anyone but the wealthier families in the school. Each week there are announcements over the PA system. "Freddie Heimstra is the week's top seller," or "Mary Metros wins this week's drawing." The only way to win a prize, to get announced over the PA, or get your name in the drawing is to hit the streets and sell some raffle tickets.

I am describing the perfect motivation for a grade school kid, especially me in the fourth grade (see Figure I.2).

Recognition in front of your peers. Prizes your family would never give you unless it was Christmas, and even then, it would be a family gift, not yours. It's a chance to win something just for participating. To control my destiny.

I am motivated. This year's prizes include a new electronic toy, the Mattel Football handheld game. At the time I have three channels of television, only a handful of Saturday morning shows to watch, and these

Figure I.2 Fourth-grade Greg

Mattel Football games are advertised at every commercial break. It's hard to describe how much I want this toy. I not only want the toy, I want the recognition. I want to have my name in lights. I can imagine getting recognized for being the number one seller at the festival. I am ascending the gym stage to a standing ovation and stop for just a beat to feel the adulation of my adoring fans. I turn to the side and the parish priest, with a tear in his eye, mouths, "Bless you, top seller."

Even now I can almost taste it.

My tickets are handed to me on the first Friday of the fund raiser. Three bunches of five tickets each. We are given instructions on how to process the order, the buyer gets this part of the ticket, the school get this part, return the cash and the completed stubs to the office on Monday. I'm ready. The carpool drops me off, I check in at home, power down an after-school snack, and hit the neighborhood.

I know my route—next door are the Cunninghams, then the Richards, then some grouchy old people, then the young couple with the big dog, then the McCartys whose seven boys go to public school where there are no fund raisers, then the old couple with a nice yard. Across the street are families with girls about my age, but I don't know anything about them. It's a neighborhood where everyone knows everyone else. It should be easy pickings.

With confidence I ring the first bell. Nothing. I ring the second where Mark Richards tells me his parents will be home later, and asks if we're playing ball. I skip the old man's house, and walking up to next house, see the big dog in the bay window. Cujo is not happy to see me on his turf and looks like he's going to come through the bay window, so I make haste to the McCartys'. Eric McCarty is my age and answers the door. His mom is asleep (nurse working the night shift). I explain what I'm doing, he tells me it's dumb, I agree, and we go get Mark to start a game of Whiffle Ball.

No sustained action. No tickets sold. Motivation gone.

Each day for the next couple of weeks, I walk past the trophy case on my way out of school and see the Mattel game, lighting a fire under my belt before I leave. Yet when I get home I never go out selling tickets. A few friends say they sold tickets to grandparents and other relatives, but no one I know earns the prizes. On the bus, an older boy, Chris Fusik, has won but his dad has an office, he tells us, so selling tickets is as easy as putting up a sign on the front desk. Lucky guy.

As the festival draws near, I get my parents involved. With my mom standing backup at the curb, I head back into the neighborhood and go from door to door. As it happens, some classmates live in the same neighborhood, so most households are done buying tickets. On the last day, my dad begrudgingly takes out his checkbook and buys my allotted tickets.

Motivation can only do so much. It can spark us to action, but after that we need something to help us stay in motion, overcoming the inevitable obstacles and friction ahead.

Focusing on Momentum

In the fourth grade I am in motion and have a little momentum heading into the first obstacle I encounter, but something as small as a Wiffle Ball brings me to a halt. Physics describes momentum as:

$$p = mv, \text{ or roughly, Momentum} = \text{Mass} \times \text{Velocity}$$

I may have had some energy hiding in my little bit of fourth grader mass, but without speed I did not stay in motion long.[1] Too many friction points.

This equation is meaningful for our day-to-day work in sales. Momentum helps us overcome obstacles. Because guess what? Sales is nothing but obstacles. Prospects telling us no. Buyers who are not who they say they are. Competition beating us to the punch. Commission plans that don't make any sense. If all we do to push through resistance is use more motivation to create even more motion, but we don't remove obstacles, most of us give up long before we win. We'll tell ourselves the prize isn't worth it. The effort is too much. We'll convince ourselves other people are only successful because they're lucky.

In this book, we're not going to think about motivation. Yep, we're going to do our best to ignore it. Instead, we'll tell ourselves that since we got out of bed and showed up to work, we're motivated enough.

---

[1] At the risk of spreading disinformation, I'll stay away from the physics equations for the rest of the book.

With motivation off to the side, we're going to get into the business of focusing on the process behind generating momentum, getting on a hot streak. *The Sales Momentum Mindset* we'll call it. We'll dig deeper into how we should think about Momentum and we'll harness a Sales Momentum Mindset by considering what keeps it from happening. We'll address both the personal and organizational obstacles we can control, and we'll end by considering tactics and techniques for building both personal momentum and team momentum.

If you have questions or comments along the way, contact me at greg@chamberspivot.com. I promise to get back to you as fast as I can.

Let's light this candle.

Where I'm Coming From

This book is not the culmination of decades of research, or a summary of other painstakingly gathered tests and conclusions. It is a collection of my own observations that lack proper controls and objectivity. It is, to put it simply, the sum of observations and conversations from a guy who "loves to watch people," they say.

Through these observations, I've come to imagine our momentum as an internal flywheel. This can be a 10- or 50-pound flywheel. I see it as the big wheel on one of those old-timey bicycles. The penny-farthing (see Figure I.3). The effort it takes to get this contraption going depends on a lot of things, including having the rider in balance, the wheel on a stable axle, and outsiders keeping an eye out for obstacles.

As a new sales manager, I felt like Sisyphus, tasked with getting a bunch of these crazy bikes up the hill. What worked one day, wouldn't

Figure I.3 Penny-farthing flywheels

work the next. I'd get their bikes to the crest of the hill, only to see them fall over and bounce back to the bottom, over and over. I prodded those riders, coaxed the riders, threatened the riders, pleaded with them, and in the end figured out getting those crazy bikes up the hill was the wrong way to approach the problem. The riders were going to ride to the best of their ability. I needed to quit worrying about motivation and just point whatever momentum they generated in the same direction as the company's goals. From that point on, everyone's job got easier.

You will find this book is full of little stories because, as someone who loves to watch people, I see our little stories as the easiest way for us to understand new ideas. These stories should remind you of your own experiences and let you imagine what it's like to see the world less through the lens of motivation and more through the lens of momentum.

I'll limit the stories to my experiences helping these crazy bicycles get moving, restarting a rider that's come to rest, and how to make your wheel larger so momentum carries you further than it ever has before. It's worked for me. It's worked for my teams. It works for my clients, and it will work for you.

PART 1

The Big Question

If Motivation Isn't the Solution, Why Do We Spend So Much Time Thinking About It?

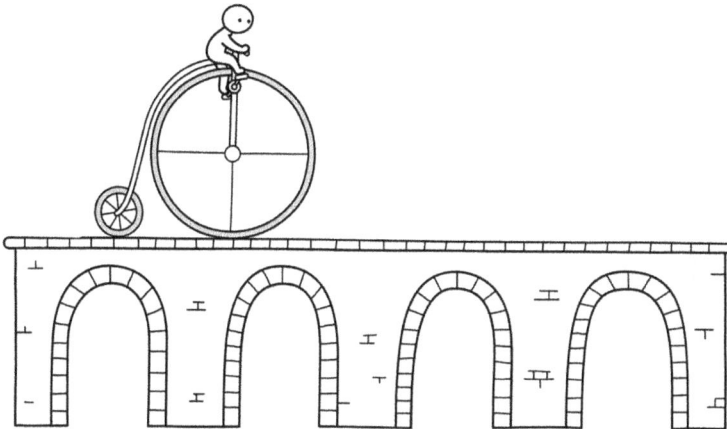

Figure P1.1 Momentum flywheel and aqueduct

CHAPTER 1

You're Motivated Enough

Overview

Salespeople and sales managers are obsessed with motivation. However, what we think of as motivation is really inspiration, which, while it may bring short-term results, doesn't give us long-term results. Long-term results come from another kind of motivation called continuity. The way to get from inspiration to continuity is momentum.

It may sound like a hot take, but I think you're already motivated enough. I think your people are motivated enough. As my mentor Mr. Carl[1] would say, "Gregory, if you are showing up to work each day sober, rested, and on-time you're 90 percent of the way to success." If we discard Mr. Carl's penchant for hyperbole, we're left with the question: if most of what it takes to be successful is to show up, why aren't we getting more done? What keeps us from doing the things we should and getting the things we want?

Here's what we're going to be thinking about for the next 150 or so pages (see Figure 1.1).

The concept of this book is that we see motivation as giving us the necessary energy to hit our sales goals, like the previous drawing. Momentum is easy. It's nothing more than putting one foot in front of the other. Step one, take step one. Then step two, three, four, … 21. Congratulations! Your momentum is now a habit and you win.

The problem is that it doesn't happen that way. There is something preventing salespeople from putting one foot in front of the other.

---

[1] The late Mr. Carl was one of my first managers, who later became a mentor. I hear his voice in my head. A lot. You'll hear what I can remember of his wisdom throughout this book.

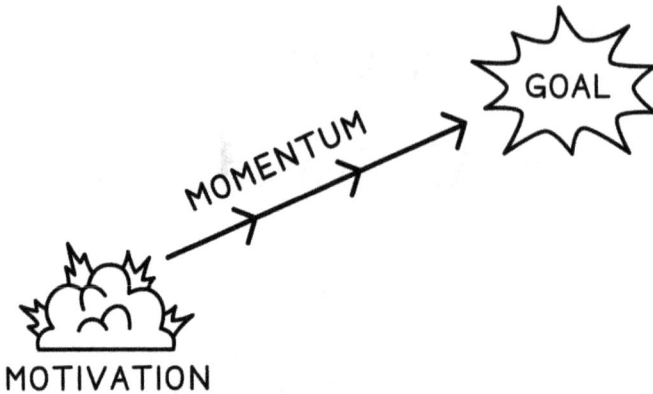

Figure 1.1 How we think motivation works

It may happen between steps one and two, or it may happen between steps 13 and 14. Something keeps us from doing what we know we should be doing, and we lose momentum.

When I talk about this problem with CEOs, business leaders, and sales managers, the solution I hear most is to add more motivation. They tell me their top people are simply more motivated than their bottom people. They hire the best and brightest, so it's not talent. Some people are more willing to put in the hours and the extra effort. They have more energy. This means management's job is all about getting their people inspired to make the effort.

Seeing performance through this lens encourages us to seek out motivational speakers, participate in rah-rah meetings, and put big, hairy, audacious goals and incentives in place.

More motivation, please!

So, why doesn't it work? In my day job, I meet with both high and low performers. As we review their activity, I've looked for evidence that motivation is driving results. Good or bad. I ask myself, do top performers have more energy? Are they in possession of some magic that low performers can't tap into? What are they doing differently? Talking about this, one Senior VP told me, "If you can show me how to motivate everyone, we can take over the world." I'm not sure if that's right.

In our time together, we're going to dig deeper into the idea: if you've shown up, you're motivated enough, so stop focusing on motivation. I will make the case that years and years of focus on motivation has not

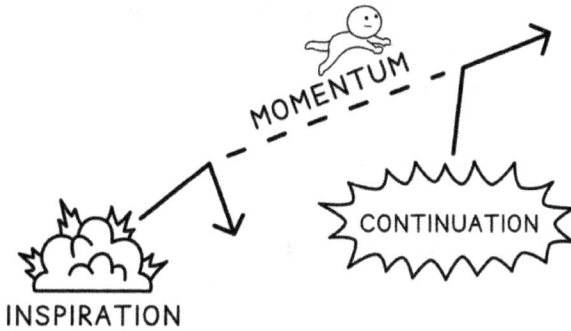

Figure 1.2 Inspiration, momentum, continuation

led to sustained success or "taking over the world." On the other hand, if we leave motivation behind and focus on Momentum, something interesting happens.

We see that early motivation, often called *Inspiration*, gets us up and moving, but this inspiration doesn't correlate to success (see Figure 1.2). After inspiration fades, it's momentum that keeps us moving toward our goal. Small day-to-day activities, putting one foot in front of another. Then, as Momentum builds, another interesting thing happens. Motivation reappears. This new motivation doesn't sound like Inspiration. And, unlike Inspiration, this type of motivation *does* correlate to success. This latter-stage motivation comes from keeping momentum going, so we'll call it *Continuation*. In this sense, top performers *are* more motivated than low performers. They have moved beyond inspiration and are now motivated to keep their momentum going. They are "respecting the streak." As one top performer told me, "Greg, I've come this far, I will do anything to keep from slipping." This motivation sounds different from rah-rah meetings or amped-up speakers on stage.

Do you remember, or did you see, the movie *"Bull Durham"*? It's about characters on a minor league professional baseball team, one heading to stardom in the Major League, the other headed to retirement. They meet as teammates on the Durham Bulls, where young up-and-coming pitcher LaRouche is starting his journey to the big leagues. The managers bring in an aging veteran to help the young, talented LaRouche get ready for life at the highest level of pro baseball. At one point, this wily veteran character, Crash Davis, gives a soliloquy about respecting the streak.

He is speaking with LaRouche's love interest (the one who, in an effort to get LaRouche to perform better, tells him to wear a pair of women's lingerie under his uniform, a very funny scene).

> Crash: "I told him that a player on a streak has to respect the streak … You know why? Because they don't—they don't happen very often … If you believe you're playing well because you're getting laid, or because you're not getting laid, or because you wear women's underwear, then you are!"[2]

Top performers respect their streaks. People who have been at the top and are no longer there understand what it felt like to be on a streak and know it isn't easy to get the magic back. People who haven't broken through don't know what the streak, a.k.a. the power of momentum, is.

This book is about how we can do a better job of harnessing a sales momentum mindset. By focusing more on momentum, we'll get closer to our goals.

Motivation: Lights Go Up, Lights Go Down

First, let's talk a little about why management is so attracted to inspirational motivation. It's because it works … to a point. In the early 20th century, as the United States moved into industrialization, a new role was being developed in businesses. These factory floors needed productivity. Henry Ford had popularized the assembly line, and a new advisory role cropped up in the business landscape. The role of a management consultant. Then, as now, there were theoretical consultants and practicing consultants. Theoretical consultants included people like Frederick Taylor, who did time and motion studies in the early factory days. Optimizing the work. His approach was basically driven by observation and a stopwatch. It makes a lot of sense. If you break a role down into small parts and focus on optimizing all the pieces, you should end up with a much more efficient system. It works for machines, why not for the people on the factory floor?

---

[2] R. Shelton, dir. 1988. *Bull Durham* Movie.

His approach promised more than it delivered, but the box had been opened, and all sorts of factories tried to make the time–motion approach work. It's unfair to say the idea had no merit; it had some effectiveness some of the time. It was sometime later that researchers from Harvard Business School[3] gave this phenomenon a name. The observations were at Western Electric's Hawthorne Works plant outside Chicago and focused on a group of women on the factory floor. They noticed that if you made the lights in the factory brighter, productivity went up. For a while. Then, within a period of time, production reverted back to the norm. Being astute scientists, they tried the opposite. What happens when you turn the lights lower than normal?

Productivity increases again!

Interesting. This is the Hawthorne effect. Changing the environment in any number of ways causes a temporary burst of productivity before work settles back to its previous level, what we call reverting to the norm.[4]

This is what happens with Inspiration. Hire a motivational speaker and get a burst of activity. I haven't heard of anyone doing this, but according to the Hawthorne effect, it stands to reason that hiring a demotivational speaker will get the same result. Either way, this increased activity is not going to last. It's there for a short time and then goes away.

When I worked in an inside sales call-center, I saw the Hawthorn effect in person. We'd spend late nights coming up with creative ways to incent the sales force, once even sourcing giant-sized Publisher's Clearinghouse Sweepstakes checks for monthly contests. We'd bring out the check with balloons and confetti, take pictures, and blast loud music. The first time we did it, no one knew what to expect. The second time, people fought to get recognition, and sales increased. This boost in sales

---

[3] "A Field Is Born." July 1, 2008. *Harvard Business Review*. https://hbr .org/2008/07/a-field-is-born. In the 1920s, Harvard Business School professors Elton Mayo and Fritz J. Roethlisberger studied worker behavior at Western Electric's Hawthorne Works plant outside Chicago.

[4] S.D. Levitt and J.A. List. May 28, 2009. "Was There Really a Hawthorne Effect at the Hawthorne Plant? An Analysis of the Original Illumination Experiments." www.nber.org. www.nber.org/papers/w15016. Levitt and List found the effect is "far more subtle than previously acknowledged." For our purposes, it describes the effect we see when we intensify motivational techniques.

would work for a few more months, but by the fifth month, no one seemed to care. By the sixth month, even the sales managers were bored with the program. Before you knew it, we'd settle right back into our old levels of production.

We'd try another tactic. What about a trip to the Caymans? What about a new watch? What about no contests for a quarter after firing the bottom 10 percent of producers? My comanager called it "keeping the team edgy," and it worked.

But it never lasted long. That darn Hawthorne effect.

The problem with relying on what my friend called "keeping people on edge" is that it gets tougher over time. We humans are incredibly adaptable. The celebratory recognition worked once. Maybe twice. By the third time we tried it, everyone was on board with us. No edge, no jump in sales.

This is the problem with focusing on inspiration to boost sales. The first speaker will be dynamite, with her impact lasting for weeks or months. The second will be good, and their impact may last a week. The third will result in little to no change. It's how we are as people. This isn't just a U.S.-centric phenomenon, either. It's a worldwide phenomenon.

This isn't to say inspiration and motivational techniques won't work. I'm here to tell you that they do work. What I'm saying is that there is an approach you can take that will have a longer-lasting impact on performance, especially if you are in a sales role. If you're a manager, this focus will have a longer-lasting effect on your team's performance.

Focus on building and sustaining momentum.

The Seller's Bias: My Default Lens

I have my own work experience with motivation, what you might call a throughline. To explain what I mean by throughline, let me take you back a few years. To jump-start my sales activity, I attended a conference of consultants. It's inspirational to surround yourself with high-performing people who do the same things you do. Some of the consultants who spoke at this conference trained us on their expertise, with others serving as inspirational plenary speakers on the theme of the conference. All the speakers were incredibly good, and every single one motivated me. But one speaker stood out.

She did a crazy mime act as part of her speech. You know, mime acting like they're stuck in a box kind of thing. I don't know how you feel about mimes. I personally don't think of them often, maybe never, but I know people have strong reactions to them, including hatred.[5] This speaker was the opposite; she loved the art form. She studied under master mime, Marcel Marceau, and her talk included minutes dedicated to the audience watching her mimic a dying seagull, among other things. Odd, but memorable. Her talk's theme has stuck with me for years. It was about throughlines.

She described throughlines as the central theme of our work or lives. For instance, the throughline running through her life was expressing herself through art, including physical expressions of art like miming. In this sense, motivation has, up to now, been the default sales and selling throughline for me and millions of other salespeople.

I now think of throughlines as our default state of being. We have certain core behaviors we've cultivated through years of practice. In sales, most of us have bought into the idea of being motivated. It makes sense because it takes energy and effort to get through a dozen no's to get to a yes, and the best way to work up the energy for overcoming obstacles, we've learned, is to pump ourselves up. We look for inspiration. The throughline, or default state, for sales is inspiration.

This is me. I love a good pump-up session. If push comes to shove and I'm at a loss for what to do next, my knee-jerk response is motivation. I want to make a dream board, set a big hairy audacious goal, imagine a life of riches, visualize running through the tape in the first place, and everything else. I love motivation.

The thing is, as I've moved from direct sales to sales management, and to leadership roles outside of sales, constantly motivating and coming up with new ways to get more from myself and my people, I've come to a conclusion.

---

[5] T. Vitale, C. Woloshin, and A. Bourdain. 2012. *Review of the Layover: Paris.* Celebrity chef Anthony Bourdain was a mime hater. His crew brought a mime to him in this episode. Of the incident he said, "I have post-mime stress disorder. Every time from now on I see a striped shirt I'm going to clench."

We don't need to focus on motivation. It's already there.

I'm not the only one to think this. It turns out a professional football player had the same idea. I heard it while listening to Aaron Rodgers, the future hall of fame NFL quarterback of the Green Bay Packers (now with the New York Jets). He was in contract negotiations with his team, and before the 2021 season, he held a press conference. In that press conference, he said something that got my head nodding, solidifying what I've been talking about for a long time now.

Good things happen when you forget about motivation.

He was responding to a question from a reporter about his leadership in the locker room, and he quoted a fellow NFL player, Darren Perry, to describe his approach:

"True motivation ultimately comes from within."

I thought, yes! This is what I've been saying. If you show up to work every day, you're motivated enough. As a matter of fact, I wanted to title this book "*Just Motivated Enough*" because if you get to the office each day and if your people get to the office each day, that's all you need. They're motivated enough to do the work. If we accept that motivation is taken care of, we can focus on making it easier to get the work done.

My default has been, and will always be, motivation-oriented. I love standing up in front of people and getting them fired up. The thing is, even when I'm doing it, I know it won't work long term. It's the Hawthorne effect. When a VP of Sales asks if I can come in and give the team some words of inspiration, I say yes. I can make you feel good, and I can inspire your team, but I tell her that in six months there is likely to be little or no change in performance. The regression to the mean will have happened, and it will be like I was never there.

Let's fix this. Instead of telling ourselves we need to get motivated or find some inspiration, let's tell ourselves we need to get better at building momentum. We need to continue what inspiration puts into motion.

We need to respect the streak.

Why This Works: The Three Types of Salespeople

The world operates in threes, doesn't it? So, it's no surprise that I think the people who find themselves in sales fit into one of three broad categories.

Whether you're in a direct production role or a supervisory role, the importance of these definitions is that they help transition us from our default motivation/inspiration lens to ones bathing the world in the light of momentum. Let me give you some brief definitions before explaining their importance.[6]

- **A Natural:** The extrovert who has always been told they should be in sales.
- **A Realist:** The means-to-an-end person in sales because they must do something for work.
- **A Dreamer:** The vision-driven person.

The first group, the *Naturals*, is the default image the man on the street has of salespeople. Naturally gregarious, they are extroverts, competitive, and driven to do their best. At some point, someone in their life probably said to them, "You should be in sales because you like talking to people." The key features of this group include that they don't mind getting out and talking to new people, they enjoy the idea of being paid for performance, and they like the time freedoms in the job. In my experience, there are 20 to 25 percent of salespeople who fit this description.

The second group, the *Realists*, is populated with people who ended up in sales versus choosing it. I fall into this group. There's an old saying in business, "Nothing happens until something gets sold." The factory won't go to work, the back office won't push papers, and the managers will have no one to tell them what to do if the orders aren't coming in. It's a simplistic view of business, but it explains why there are so many sales-related roles to fill. With most people not knowing what they want to do with their lives, needing to make a living, and ready to end the job search, they take a job in sales. I needed to make some money; the best-paying positions were in sales, and the rest is history. The feature of this group is not so much their love of sales work as the fact that a sales job fills a

---

[6] "Your Sales Training Is Probably Lackluster. Here's How to Fix It." June 12, 2017. *Harvard Business Review*. In 2017 it was estimated U.S. companies spend over $70BN in sales training. The same study showed 80 percent of the training was forgotten within 90 days. Sounds like the Hawthorne effect.

need in their lives. Once they start in sales, the earning potential of other jobs pales in comparison, and this keeps them in sales roles. With good management, this group is filled with strong producers, but the manager makes a big difference. Side note: If you have to pull a sales manager from a selling role, these people are perfect because they are naturally plugged into thinking about sales as a process.

The last group of people in sales, the dreamers, often don't call themselves salespeople. They like to be referred to as dealmakers or rainmakers, or maybe business development people, but they "aren't in sales." They have strong feelings for the work their firms are doing, the people they work with, or the customers they are working for. You can say this group is mission driven because so many of them are. They are focused on the firm's success or the customer's success, and to get performance, their manager only needs to remind them of that. They'll get the work done.

I mentioned the first group, which comprises 20 to 25 percent of all salespeople. The second two groups make up the rest. In some industries (health care and life sciences), you find a few more vision-driven people, but most sales teams are made of people who might have chosen a different role or might yet choose another role down the road. They are the fat parts of the bell curve.

This middle group is why a Momentum lens, the topic of this book, makes such a difference in sales. As we explore the ways to build momentum, the ways to lose momentum, and how to sustain and regain momentum, it's this middle group, the largest group, that is impacted the most. The first group thinks of the world as sales, the last group has a purpose, and the middle group, well, the middle group is happy to have a job. If the job can be made a little better through a combination of internal and environmental factors, all the better.

Shifting Attention: The Pareto Principle, Flipped

The Naturals drive the behaviors we see in the modern sales force. They get excited about new opportunities and like the emotional transfer that happens when they implement inspirational tactics. Since they gravitate toward the role of salesperson, they hover in the top half of sales production. Top producers dominate sales cultures, and this is why we see the most effort going to what they want: inspiration.

Have you heard of the Pareto principle? It's a mathematical hypothesis that is loosely defined as getting 80 percent of the results from 20 percent of the sample size (see Figure 1.3). When it comes to motivation versus momentum, I think of that 20 percent. We spend 80 percent of our time on motivation; we don't notice the little effort we put into building, maintaining, or rebuilding momentum. Here's the thing Pareto suggested to us all those years ago: this 20 percent invested in momentum is probably giving us 80 percent of the results we get out of sales. It's not 80 percent of the time we spend on motivation.

What happens when we invest 40–50–60 or even 80 percent of our time on momentum? Motivation is still there. The Naturals still pick up motivational books, the Realists still mimic the Naturals, and the Dreamers still tell stories about the good work they are doing. Our current results won't be affected. There's no reason not to spend our time thinking about momentum. Make the switch on purpose; do it most of the time. Give it a name to harness its power.

After I explained this concept to one business owner, he said, "I just got goosebumps when you said that." Goosebumps I associate with motivational speaking, not momentum, but he explained more.

> Greg, as you just said, I think we do momentum already and just don't know it. We preach about trusting the process and how to make it easier to sell more, but we don't do it on purpose. And we don't have language for it. I think you're on to something.

20% EFFORT

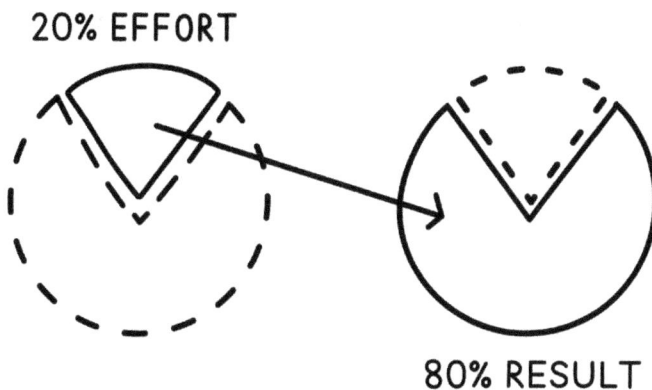

80% RESULT

Figure 1.3 The Pareto principle

This is where the book in your hands, *"The Sales Momentum Mindset,"* comes from. We're going to get deeper into momentum and give ourselves a language and framework to work within. You'll find, as I have, that momentum ideas cross borders, cultures, and industries because they are rooted in being human, something we all have experience with.

Good Stuff in Chapter 1

When you look at people who are successful, you will find that they aren't the people who are motivated but have consistency in their motivation.

—Arsene Wenger, legendary Arsenal football club manager

- You're already motivated enough because it's the default setting for sales. Ignoring motivation and focusing on momentum increases activity and improves results faster. In the battle between being good and being there, in sales, it's always better to be there. Momentum makes sure you're out there.
- What we think of as motivation is usually Inspiration, which doesn't produce long-term results. The type of motivation producing long-term results is Continuity. The bridge between them is Momentum. When we don't get the results we want it's usually an interruption in momentum, not a lack of inspiration, that's the culprit.
- Whether you're in sales because you're a Natural, a Realist, or a Dreamer, ignoring questions of motivation and concentrating on momentum will increase your sales. This is because momentum forces us to figure out why we are or aren't in motion, keeping us moving.
- The best part about focusing on building momentum on purpose is what starts out as conscious effort becomes unconscious behavior. It doesn't take long (but it does take concentrated effort to start).

CHAPTER 2

Momentum for the Win

Overview

Momentum is the bridge between two kinds of motivation, inspiration and continuation. To get the long-term success that comes with continuation, ignore inspiration and focus on the concepts driving momentum. Internal momentum concepts like Discipline, Humanity, Surrendering, and Navigation. External concepts like Vision, Incentives, Culture, and Change.

In this chapter we're going to cover definitions and tools. This will help us develop our language around momentum. Before we do that, however, I'm going to pick on motivation for a minute more. Once I started questioning top performers across organizations: the high-performing salespeople, the best rainmakers, the executives marshalling support for their organizations, and the startup evangelists, I heard a phrase repeated in one way or another as the answer for what is driving their success.

I've come this far; I need to keep going.

This doesn't sound like the motivation I know. It doesn't sound like the guy busting out of bed, knocking out his stretches and crowing, at the top of his lungs, "I'm alive! I'm awake! And I feel great!" His young family rising, bleary eyed out of their slumber to admire the effort their old man is going to put in today.

No, it sounds more like people are excited about, yet somewhat resigned to, doing a good day's work. I talk to salespeople about what they think is most important to success: having a purpose, money motivation, accolades, or something else? What I learn is there are as many answers as there are people I ask. As a matter of fact, asking the same people the same question on different days gives me different answers.[1] It's no wonder company executives and managers throw up their hands. "Greg, just come in and tell my people an inspirational story and get them going." It works as well as anything and we know why: it's the Hawthorne effect. For short-term results, something is better than nothing.

How do we get away from defaulting to inspiration and bridge into this more permanent motivation of our top performers?

It's a big question, with a simple answer. Shift our focus from motivation to thinking about momentum. Change the lens we're looking through. Think of the old lens of motivation as if we're wearing sunglasses near a stream on a bright, sunny day. Our eyes are shielded from the sun's glare, but the light bouncing off the uneven surface of the stream makes it hard to see anything but moving water. Not a problem on most days, but if you're trying to catch a fish in the stream, it's a problem.

Changing to a momentum lens, on the other hand, brings the world into sharp focus. It's like switching from our regular sunglasses to a pair of polarized lenses. Suddenly, the glare from the ripples in the stream is gone. We can see the rocks in the stream, we can see the pockets where fish hang out, and we can see those trout looking for food. The good news is you have these polarized momentum lenses inside you, right now. Every salesperson and manager talks about elements of momentum; they just don't use the lens on purpose. This happens everywhere. My friends in Australia, Spain, Ireland, and Germany confirm it. If I knew people in South America, Africa, and Asia I'm sure they'd confirm it too. We know momentum, we just don't focus on it. Let's change this.

The Second Motivation: Inspiration Then Continuation

Look at Figure 2.1. The first thing we're going to do is keep motivation in a section of our toolbox where we can see and use it. Let's go back to that Aaron Rodgers quote. Motivation comes from within. When we use

---

[1] Searching for salesperson motivation on the *Harvard Business Review* brings up hundreds of results. Finding the exact right motivation is not a new problem. The good news is whatever the advice, it works ... for a time.

MOTIVATION   MOMENTUM

Figure 2.1 Group motivation versus momentum

a momentum lens it's easy to see. You got up, got out of bed, dragged a comb across your head, and started the day. That's what inspiration does. It gets you into the game. Mr. Carl was right—showing up, working, and staying sober are all the motivation you need. The rest is taking action and trying to build momentum.

Our internal motivation gets us to take the first few steps; then it's your job to take even more steps. Momentum is mass × velocity over time. Mass, velocity, and time working together enable you to get to continuation whatever it is you're doing, in whatever direction you're going.

Bicycle marketers know this. I used to sell bicycles. Part of selling bicycles is low pay but a grubby kind of glamour. To compensate for this, the bicycle companies have what are called "pro-deals." They will sell people in the industry their products at cost. They won't let you buy much more than a piece or two, but it's a perk. You get the newest and best stuff. Customers see you in the good stuff, and they want to buy it.

When I was in the bike business, I took advantage of a pro-deal. It was on a new type of mountain bike with 27" or 700-cc wheels. At that point most mountain bikes used 26" wheels. They were sturdier, and when riding on trails you didn't need the smooth ride a bigger wheel gives you. This company's marketers sold me on the idea that a bigger wheel rolled over obstacles easier. They sold me on the idea my momentum wouldn't be interrupted. If I could get my mass up to speed, a rock that may interrupt the momentum of a guy on a 26" set of wheels would roll under my giant 27" wheels like any old pebble.

Is it true? I have no idea. It's marketing and I liked the story. I still tell it. I still have the bike too! It's a monster, and whenever I see an obstacle coming, I think, "I got this," and roll right over it.

This brings up another point everyone in sales knows. Perception is reality. If I perceive the larger-wheeled mountain bike is rolling more smoothly over obstacles, it is my reality. It's the way it is. We'll talk about using perception to our advantage in a minute, but for now my goal is to get you to say to your standard issue motivation lens, "I love you, I respect you, but I'm going to put a little more emphasis on another part of my work life right now."

We're going to see the world through the lens of momentum.

Momentum Tools: Storytelling

A housekeeping bit here. Let's talk about Storytelling, A Few Good People, and Harnessing Energy. These are ingredients in the mortar we'll be using to put the building blocks of momentum together.

First up are **Stories**. We relate to the world through stories, especially in sales, because selling is communication, and stories are how we like to communicate. This book will use stories as much as possible because you'll find stories effective in changing lens from motivation to momentum.

Storytelling is so powerful a technique for how we see the world, it's even been shown to distort memory. Our memories are really nothing more than the stories we tell ourselves. For example, do you remember the saga of NBC Nightly News anchor Brian Williams?[2] In the mid 2000s, he was arguably the most famous television news anchor in the United States. As part of his duties, he ran all over the world visiting natural disasters and war-torn regions. In one of these visits his team was exiting their helicopter and came under fire from an enemy. It was a harrowing experience for everyone involved. A near-death event leaving scars on the participants for years to come. Brian Williams told the story time

---

[2] A.E. Nutt. February 2015. "The Science Behind Brian Williams's Mortifying Memory Flub," *The Washington Post*.

and time again as an illustration of just how harrowing a journalist's job could be.

The thing is, it never happened. Brian Williams was telling himself a story.

There are critics of the media who point to this storytelling as evidence of why you can't trust the media, but the researchers who study memory won't go that far. They will tell us that it's entirely possible Mr. Williams really believed he was there, in that helicopter taking on sniper fire, each time he told the story. The reason he believed it to be true is because we don't form memories the way most people think.

We think of our brains as a hard drive where the day's events, our memories, are written and stored. In reality, when we remember an event, we are engaging our brain in remembering the story we told before.

I tease my mother about this all the time. She remembers things from my youth and young adulthood that definitely never happened. Other times she shares memories of stories I've told, my stories, things she's only heard about, but she tells the story as if it were her own. Just like Brian Williams. I do the same. We all do.

This is why storytelling is your best ally for changing your lens to momentum to improve results. As you read this book you will be reminded of times in your sales career, or management career, or business life in general, where momentum carried you through. Or where focusing on keeping momentum led you to impressive results. Grab on to those memories. Tell those stories. Over and over and over. Because not only is it important to share information via stories, it's also important to repeat these stories again and again. Build momentum with repetition if you will.

This is how we communicate the impact of momentum in our life and the lives of those around us.

Momentum Tools: A Few Good People

The next element in our mortar mix for the building blocks of momentum is the idea of A Few Good People.

Do you know what makes a good leader? A good follower. A good leader doesn't need everyone to follow them to be effective; they just need one follower to get things going.

Have you ever seen the video of the one guy dancing on the hill at the Sasquatch! Music Festival?[3] The video is of one guy doing a weird drugged-out, arms-flailing, messy dance on the side of a hill at a festival. All alone. For quite some time. It's funny and a little sad.

Then someone jumps into the area and starts dancing with him. That's all it takes. Once the second person comes in it's less than a minute before the third, fourth, and fifth people come in. Soon this dancing man has formed a little dancing militia. You can't even see him anymore.

Keep this in mind when you are implementing the elements of momentum. Whether you're in sales and looking for an advantage or in management and trying to elevate your team, it all starts with one. One person talking about momentum. All the time.

Because it has to be all the time, right? We know this from storytelling. One person committed to repeating the dance over and over and over. This leads to two people, then four.

It will happen and we'll talk about how to get it there.

When you find one person working on momentum, run with it. Harness their energy. Help them build momentum.

Momentum Tools: Harnessing Energy

The third ingredient in changing our lens from motivation to momentum involves harnessing energy where you find it. Mr. Carl used to say, start anywhere, go everywhere. What he was telling me is I need to get good at recognizing where the energy is and spend time there. It's easier to work with an object in motion than it is to get a stationary object moving.

In this book we're going to talk about a lot of separate concepts, and it will feel like there is no way to account for everything listed. It's true. One of the great things about momentum, which we'll talk about in detail in Chapter 11, is momentum doesn't need to last forever for it to be effective.

Let me say that again: **momentum doesn't need to last forever for it to be effective.**

---

[3] If you haven't seen it, it's worth the 3:05 running time. https://youtu.be/GA8 z7f7a2Pk.

This is a big concept. Motivation is talked about like it's something the greats have and keep. We know this isn't true.

Let me give you an example. In sales we use a lot of sports analogies, and one of my favorite analogies is the game of golf. When you look at the Professional Golf Association (PGA) tour scores over many rounds you find that during a season the top golfers are not separated from the bottom golfers by all that much. You might think this leads to anyone taking any one week's golf prize home because they're all amazing, so everyone has a chance. I get that.

But what about the top winning golfers, the ones who win multiple big titles in their careers? They're different, right?

What if I told you that among major golf tournament winners, the majority of the multi-Major winners won their titles in bursts of dominance. You're thinking, well, what about Tiger? What about Niklaus? What about Mickelson? They stick out for a reason. I'm looking at the full list of multi-Major winners. A lot of them picked up their titles in a burst of production, not consistently over decades. These names include some of the greatest names in golf: Johnny Miller, Curtis Strange, Bubba Watson, Jordan Spieth, and others.

All won multiple majors inside 24-month periods.

The thing is, it's not just professional golf. This pattern shows up in professors publishing important papers. It shows up with mutual fund managers. It shows up in education. I saw a study of private equity deals repeating this same pattern.[4]

The thing they all have in common is they are not producing exceptional results year in, year out for their whole career. They get on a roll, they get the momentum going, it lasts for a period of time, and that's all it takes to make their mark.

---

[4] L. Liu, Y. Wang, R. Sinatra, C.L. Giles, C. Song, and D. Wang. 2018. "Hot Streaks in Artistic, Cultural, and Scientific Careers," *Nature* 559, no. 7714, pp. 396–399 and S.K. Ram, S. Nandan, and D. Sornette. 2020. "Significant Hot Hand Effect in International Cricket," *SSRN* 3644211. Hot streaks are identified as periods during which someone's performance is significantly better than usual. They found this pattern among artists, film directors, scientists, and sports performers.

What does this have to do with harnessing energy? Meet people where they are. Meet yourself where you stand today. Whatever part of your life is working well, use that to practice some of these techniques and tactics. Don't demand perfection, just get started. Momentum begets momentum as they say.

Our Framework: The Momentum Flywheel

If you're like me, it helps to have a mental image of a framework before jumping into the details. When I first started talking to the people I coached or the organizations I consulted with about the role of momentum, I started with a group focus instead of working on individuals first. As a coach friend of mine would say, we should always aim for "less finger, more thumb" (see Figure 2.2).

(To get the full effect, when you say "less finger," point your pointer finger at some target in the distance you'd like to blame and shake your head side to side, and when you say "more thumb," point your thumb to your chin and nod your head up and down). It's a great way of saying let's start with ourselves and model the change we want in the world. No need to demand the world change when we can get a lot done by changing our internal lens first.

My first ideas on momentum focused on sales managers getting a team to goal. If motivation is pushing and pulling salespeople toward the

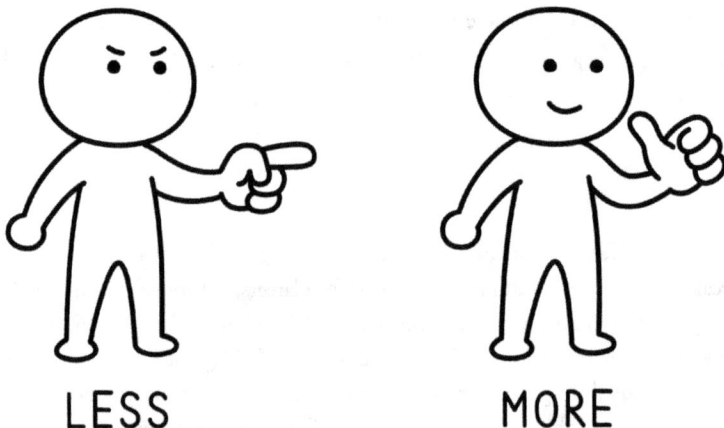

LESS   MORE

Figure 2.2 The finger and the thumb

target, momentum, I said, tells sales managers to stop the push/pull and, instead, keep the path cleared. Getting things out of our team's way, so to speak.

I'd tell them about the research.[5] Default sales inspiration is what the scientists call provocative motivation (inspiration). It's the jolt to get up and get going toward something. Those same scientists noticed that when they studied this motivation, it changed as the subjects made progress toward their goal. It moved from provocative, moving toward a goal, and became conservative. The subjects, once moving, were now motivated not to lose the progress they made.

I'd tell clients that this is what a change in lenses will do for us. We will start thinking of momentum as conserving the energy that's been generated, rather than generating new energy.

Some of those explanations worked, but it fell flat when we tried to put it to work. It wasn't a framework. It was too externally focused. Things changed when we stopped looking at the team as a whole and started to look inside ourselves. First we started asking, what can we as individuals do to conserve our momentum? Then, what could the firm do for momentum?[6]

The wheel you see in Figure 2.3 is divided into four segments and it represents what we can do as individuals. Or rather, it represents the forces inside us that represent the mass we'll turn into energy over time. It has concepts that are Discipline-related like health and wealth, concepts like Surrender that depend on others like support systems and community, and concepts that help us Navigate like mentors and hidden rules.

Get all these concepts in order and you tend to build momentum, rolling forward, effectively. When you hit an obstacle, your momentum carries you over it. Conversely, when these concepts are out of balance, it

---

[5] S.E. Iso-Ahola and C.O. Dotson. August 2016. "Psychological Momentum—a Key to Continued Success," *Frontiers in Psychology* 7. https://doi.org/10.3389/fpsyg.2016.01328.

[6] This book owes a huge debt of gratitude to Dr. Ruby K. Payne's book, *A Framework for Understanding Poverty*. (R.K. Payne. 2019. *A Framework for Understanding Poverty: A Cognitive Approach for Educators, Policymakers, Employers, and Service Providers*. Highlands, TX: Aha! Process, Inc.)

Figure 2.3 The momentum flywheel

can make momentum hard to get started. Even tiny obstacles bring your wheel to a halt.

This doesn't mean momentum is only up to us as individuals. The road we're running on makes a difference too (see Figure 2.4). When we thought about the firm (our companies/organizations), we saw ways they could encourage or discourage momentum and we started thinking of it as a bridge carrying us from inspiration to continuation. It has concepts like clarity of vision, which I outlined in my book "*The Human Being's*

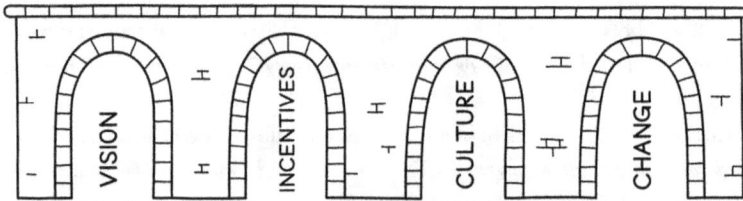

Figure 2.4 The momentum aqueduct

Guide to Business Growth"[7] (shameless plug). It led us to thinking about how incentives are structured, our co-workers' behaviors, and the firm's ability to deal with change. All of these concepts work together to build or inhibit momentum.

In the chapters that follow, we will discuss about each concept in more detail, giving us a language to use while developing our momentum lens.

As we cover each concept, it's important to install one more tool in our toolbelt. The wheel and the bridge are great, stories are great, but when making changes it helps to have the consultant's secret weapon at our disposal.

Subtraction Can Be More Effective Than Addition

Take a look at Figure 2.5. In coaching, we look for ways to improve the client's condition, and one of the most effective tools we have is not adding a thought into our client's heads, but in subtracting from something that's already there. As we go through the momentum exercises, I am going to present ways to both do more and do much, much less.

When I was a new sales manager, not long after I left the nest of Mr. Carl, I attended a weeklong immersive sales management training. The trainers were installing a sales management system into our heads, one with a common process and language we were using across the

Figure 2.5 Stuck between restraints and incentives

---

[7] G. Chambers 2018. *The Human Being's Guide to Business Growth: A Simple Process for Unleashing the Power of Your People for Growth* (New York, NY: BEP), pp. 37–42.

organization. It was a laudable goal and excellent training. (Although most of my colleagues joked, it was a great training for our next jobs!)

The most important piece of advice I got from this training came on the last half of the last day. We had been filled with new ideas and concepts to make ourselves better managers. We were crammed, full of innumerable sales improvement tactics, and most of us had started a detailed log of what we were going to change when we got back to the office. Since I was in one of the first groups to be trained, the trainers left us with a final instruction. There were other managers to be trained, so when we get back to the office, don't do anything different. They practiced with us on how to do nothing, and what to say when other managers and our direct reports peppered us for hints on the changes that were around the corner. There were nearly 100 managers in our company and everyone knew this sales management training was happening, so inquiring minds wanted to know what to expect. "Please keep quiet," the trainers said. Give us another two months to get everyone on the same page and then we could start change very slowly.

Why was this the most important thing I took from the training? Because when I got back to my office I was changed. My lens was different and I saw my sales team in a new light. The advice to do nothing was exactly what I needed to sit back and think about what my natural instincts were (like sales-oriented thinking versus management thinking) and how to change it.

I got more from that training than any other training I've attended because I stopped behaviors that were not helping me. I took things off my plate and my personal results improved. Soon my team's results too improved.

It turns out this is a very well-known approach. I heard Nobel Prize winner Danny Kahneman[8] talk about removing behaviors being just as effective as installing new behaviors and I thought, "Yes! I've experienced that."

---

[8] In "How to Launch a Behavior Change Revolution" http://freakonomics.com/podcast/launch-behavior-change-revolution/, Daniel Kahneman said, "I'll cite the idea that, for me, is the best idea I ever heard in psychology. I heard it as an undergraduate. It's the story of how you induce people to change their behavior, as taught by Kurt Lewin. Lewin's insight was that if you want to achieve change in behavior, there is one good way to do it and one bad way to do it. The good way to do it is by diminishing the restraining forces, not by increasing the driving forces. That turns out to be profoundly non-intuitive."

In this book, we're going to talk about things we could be doing, but I encourage you to consider the idea that it may be just as easy to get to a goal by cutting restraints as it is to add. Like my little friend here. He needs to get to his goal, but he's suspended between the pull of his beliefs, his experiences, and his history holding him back. Pulling him is some proactive motivation to get him to the goal. We can either help him by doubling up on the motivation, the push and pull, or we can cut the ties that are binding him (see Figure 2.6).

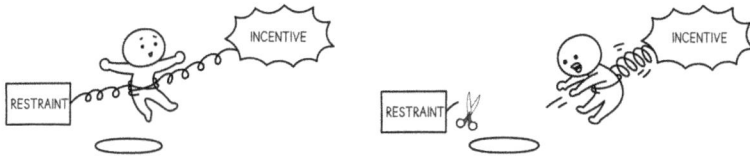

Figure 2.6 Releasing restraints

I think of my old Stretch Armstrong toy. If you were a child in the 1970s, this toy was the hottest toy on the market. I got one. We took this poor toy and pulled and pulled just like the man in the graphic. Something had to give. It wasn't going to be Stretch Armstrong. Eventually one kid would let go, both kids would fall down, and Stretch Armstrong regained his original shape. As you learn about building and maintaining momentum, keep this in mind. We can be just as effective by removing obstacles as we can by adding tactics and techniques.

In the coming chapters we're going to cover the four personal concepts, or elements of Momentum:

- Discipline Elements (Financial and Physical Well-Being)
- Humanity Elements (Emotional Control and Intellectual Firepower)
- Surrendering Elements (Support Systems and Belief in a Higher Power)
- Navigational Elements (Role Models and Knowing the Hidden Rules).

And then we'll cover the four organizational elements of Momentum:

- Vision (the company's direction)
- Incentives (the rewards for a job well done)

- Culture (the real way our companies operate)
- Change (change happens, how prepared is your company?).

Using stories, a few good people, harnessing energy, and cutting restraints, we'll have more than enough tools to help us change our lens from Inspiration to Momentum.

Good Stuff in Chapter 2

- Motivation comes in two flavors, Inspiration and Continuation. The bridge, or action, between the two is what we refer to as momentum.
- We communicate through stories, and the way you'll communicate momentum concepts to yourself and others is through the stories you choose to tell. Recognize momentum and tell stories about it.
- Not everyone needs to come along at first. Fix your new momentum lens on yourself first; others will come along as they see it work.
- Meeting people where they are and harnessing their energy is an easy way to work with friction. The myth of constant progress is just that, a myth. Harnessing energy for short sprints is much more effective.
- The parts of the momentum flywheel are Discipline, Humanity, Surrendering, and Navigation. Getting your wheel in order is the first step in harnessing a Sales Momentum Mindset.
- The parts of momentum outside your control we call the aqueduct. Our company's Vision, Incentives, Culture, and Change all have an impact on our effectiveness.
- When we start to build momentum, every little obstacle can knock us off course. As we ramp up the opposite happens. It gets hard to slow down.

PART 2

The Parts of Momentum—Inside You

Figure P2.1 *The momentum flywheel*

CHAPTER 3

The Hobgoblins of the Mind—Health and Finances

Overview

The first momentum elements we cover are internally focused. In this chapter, we take on our Discipline-related elements: Health and Finances. When we have health or financial issues, momentum is interrupted. Using preventative and contingent actions we can stay in motion and minimize the obstacles keeping us from our goals.

In the next four chapters we're going to get into more detail on the wheel. The wheel, as we touched on earlier, is about the things happening in our control (the thumb) affecting our momentum. Referring to Figure 3.1, the first two areas we're going to cover are our Financial and Physical well-being, what I call our "Discipline Elements."

Working With the Hand You're Dealt: Fortuna Is Blind

We can only deal with the hand we're dealt. Taking a cue from the ancient Romans, we're going to consider their goddess Fortuna. She is the personification of chance in everyday life. She carried a horn of plenty and wore a blindfold. As the saying goes, fortune is blind. What does this have to do with momentum? We can't spend time wishing things were different. Instead, let's focus on improving what Fortuna has given us.

Here's us humans. Little skin bags filled with chemicals and bones, trying to make it in this big bad world. We have a target, a goal, a mission, and are inspired to get there. When we set out, we find the path isn't clear and there are restraints holding us back. In Chapters 3 to 6 we're going

Figure 3.1 Discipline in the momentum flywheel

to explore four parts of momentum, each with two elements, that hold us back. When these elements are in balance, no matter what quantities we have, the rolling is easy and momentum builds. When these elements are out of balance, our progress will be slowed. Like when we have issues with discipline. When it comes to sales and selling, two areas I see having the biggest effect on momentum are in matters of Finances and in the area of Health. Areas we can get under control by exercising discipline, or self-control.

Financial Discipline: Wallet Well-Being

It's safe to say that salespeople are motivated by money. I'll go as far as saying if you're not thinking about your commission plan you may be in the wrong line of work. Now, mind you, it's possible to have top-performing salespeople that aren't motivated by the almighty dollar, pound, or rupee, but they are the exception more than the rule.

This is where we'll start in the momentum wheel. Where habits take hold. Have you heard the quote, "Habits are the hobgoblins of little minds"? Well, with the proliferation of literature about how to build habits we should focus on the number one habit that will derail a promising sales career.

Is there anything more distracting than a bill to be paid, when you don't have the money to pay it?[1]

I had the privilege of taking a group of community college students on a trip to China. We started in Shanghai. If you've had the privilege of visiting this amazing city, you might agree with me when I tell people it's like visiting the future. The city is electric. We checked into our hotel, The Shanghai Hotel (pro tip, there are a lot of "Shanghai Hotels"; grab the business card on the counter to show to taxi drivers). I grabbed a bunch of kids and said, let's do this, let's explore Shanghai. I peeked at the map and it looked like a couple of left turns out of the hotel would bring us right back to where we started. I didn't notice how the French Concession, as it's called, was not built on straight streets. We wandered for a while and then it was time to head back to the hotel. We had an organized tour dinner date to attend and the bus left promptly at 6 p.m.

We had taken the right number of left turns, but we were nowhere near the hotel. I took a mental note of the surrounding high-rises, of which there are many, but nothing looked familiar. Not to me or to any of my party of young, out-of-their-element students. The majority of whom had just been on their first international flight. This group was green and looking to me for guidance, but there was a problem.

I was lost.

It turns out the left turns I was taking were on curved streets, leading us further and further from our hotel. We were really lost. The group sensed it and grew very agitated. I figured it was no big deal because there were a few English speakers on the route and people help people in need. This is the reason I'm telling you this story. Not everyone has this point

---

[1] There is a significant association between worrying about finances and distress: S. Ryu and L. Fan. 2023. "The Relationship Between Financial Worries and Psychological Distress Among U.S. Adults," *Journal of Family and Economic Issues* 44, no. 1, pp. 16–33.

of view. Some of us walk through life on a literal razor's edge, expecting bad things to happen. When we got lost, I learned some of the students had no money to get lost on. After a dozen missteps, we were rescued at a Howard Johnsons (which in China was a luxury hotel!), where we found an English speaker who found the "Shanghai Hotel" we were staying at and arranged three cabs. With the exchange rate each cab ride came to approximately U.S.$2.50 but that was lost on my group. They had a very strict budget, it was day one, we were in a VERY foreign country, and getting lost was bad.

This trip reinforced the idea momentum can be killed in a hurry by a perceived lack of funds.

I put financial security first in this book because when I look back on working with salespeople, even some of the most talented salespeople I've known, if there is one place where they get knocked off track, it is finances.

As a sales manager, you have little or nothing to do with your employee's financial situation. If you are viewing them through a motivation lens, this isn't a problem. "Work harder and make more money," one of my early managers once told me. This advice came after I sat in his office complaining about how senior members of the sales team ditched me at a hotel bar, leaving me with an angry waitress and a $750 bill. This was in 1992, about $1,500 today. What you need to know is I had no money to my name at the time. I was a newlywed with a new baby and did not have an extra $100, let alone $1K to throw around. When I tell you finances can kill momentum, it comes from experience. I have lived these momentum-killing moments. Over and over again.

If a motivation lens showed my old sales manager it was a good idea to goose poor young Greg and tell him to try harder, a momentum lens would tell him to do something very different.

If he was seeing everything through a momentum lens, he would have recognized that his salesforce's effectiveness, his commission override, depended on seemingly minor details like a junior member's savings account. The group I supervised in China had zero room for error, no wiggle room for mistakes on a trip abroad. I had led them into a Chinese maze, and in their minds, they had very few resources to work with. They shut down. Panicked. Mind you, the start of the trip was dicey. None of us had cell service, few of our credit cards were working, and I was the only one who had successfully navigated the ATM to grab a handful of yuan. After being rescued by the HoJo concierge, the group wouldn't stop talking about it. They were rattled. My sons were on the trip, and after seeing the other travelers' reactions they said, "What's the big deal? We were lost. We figured it out."

The problem, I tried to explain, is the group did not have direct access to my resources like my boys do. They had no idea if I was going to take care of them or sell them to the highest bidder to save myself. As the trip continued, I figured out which kids had resources at their disposal, and which ones were on the trip on a wing and a prayer. These two groups' confidence levels were polar opposites of each other. It's a powerful thing to know you have what my friends call "a Mexican jail buddy." Someone you can call no matter what, no matter where you are in the world, and they'll help you solve a problem. Like, say, hypothetically being detained in a Mexican jail for some regrettable reason.

I grew up thinking everyone has these kinds of resources. I don't just have one Mexican jail friend, I have several. The kids I traveled with acted like they had no room for error.

A momentum robber.

So, what can you do about it? Everyone has their own background and risk tolerance, and it pays to take stock of your financial resource elements. If you happen to be in management, with questions you can figure out if financial resources are going to be an issue for your people.

Start with the advice most conservative financial planners give: Have an emergency fund. Most salespeople I know make better work decisions, and help their clients make better decisions when they have six months of living expenses in a cash or cash equivalent account.

You may roll your eyes at this. Some because their watch is worth more than six months of expenses, others because they can't imagine having more than a paycheck's worth of dollars sitting in their account, unaccounted for. Looking at these situations through a motivation lens, you see both a big and small bank account in one of two ways. You question their motivation. "They have a big bank account, what do they need more money for?" Or you see someone with a lot of motivation. "You want to be done living on the edge? Sell more! Get a big commission! Let's go!"

These points of view change when you flip the lens from motivation to momentum. If my old manager had this power to see momentum, he would have seen the salesperson with the big bank account and the one with zero in his account the same way, both threats to activity. He'd be focused on helping them make one more call, setting up the next appointment, and working their pipeline. He'd view both too many assets and too few assets as the same potential problem: both can kill momentum. One from lack of urgency, the other from too much urgency.

Finances are the clearest case for a momentum lens in sales. Having too big a nut to turn is just as momentum killing as having too small a nut to turn. I've coached millionaires reluctant to pick up the phone and worked with a desperately poor ex-prisoner immigrant. Motivation/ inspiration thinking makes you think they need different approaches, but momentum thinking lets you see that both individuals face the same activity problem.

Health Discipline: At Least You Have Your Health

The second part of our momentum discipline elements is health. Coming out of the pandemic, the subject of health and its impact on momentum is easy to relate to. When I say health is a key element of Momentum what I mean is when you are in good health, fit, alert, and in good spirits, momentum builds easily. When you are in bad health, out of shape, tired, and mad at the world, momentum has a hard time taking root.[2]

Early in the pandemic, before we had an effective vaccine, one of my clients brought all of his people back into the office. At the time, the concept of staying healthy and work seemed almost academic. We had endured a lockdown, but now it's time to get back to work.

The second week back, one of his people got infected. This meant the entire floor was exposed/infected. He watched helplessly as a few employees worked through bad cases of COVID while others were forced into

---

[2] M.L. Bryan, A.M. Bryce, and J. Roberts. April 2022. "Dysfunctional Presenteeism: Effects of Physical and Mental Health on Work Performance," *The Manchester School*. https://doi.org/10.1111/manc.12402.

quarantine. The same thing happened on other floors. Some employees continued to come to the office, but others refused.

He experienced first-hand how physical health impacted sales. It killed his team's momentum for two quarters. When we talked about this book, he said, "Greg, if I were thinking strictly about my people's momentum, I would have done things differently."

If it isn't easy to imagine financial discipline impacting momentum, the idea of health having an impact on momentum is easier. We only need to look at the hiring bias in big-dollar sales roles. Walk into any large trade conference where vendor booths are stretched out for miles and you'll notice the salespeople look fit and healthy. Mind you, I've never seen actual evidence equating how fit you look to your production, but that doesn't stop us from exhibiting a subconscious bias to giving the fit and vibrant person asking for a sales job preference over the out-of-shape-looking person. Outward appearances don't tell the whole story of health, but seeing the bias hiring managers have toward fit, healthy, outwardly happy people suggests deep down we know people with health issues may struggle to produce results more than people who look sick.

When I managed, we had an annual momentum-related health issue. It wasn't anything severe as the pandemic, but it impacted sales just the same.

I called it "The Super Bowl."

I knew it existed because I have been invited to Super Bowl parties from time to time. It's estimated that the day after the big game as many as 16 million people don't show up for work. In a recent survey, 26 million people admitted to showing up late or giving less than 100 percent the day after. One firm even tried to put a number on it, $6 billion in lost productivity![3]

When I was promoted as manager, I knew the Monday after the Super Bowl was going to be touch and go. Before I managed, I considered my individual production to be my private business. If I was sluggish or

---

[3] N. Lobdell. February 8, 2022. "Employers Should Expect Productivity Loss Monday After 2022 Super Bowl," *Challenger, Gray & Christmas, Inc.* www.challenger gray.com/blog/employers-should-expect-productivity-loss-monday-after-2022-super-bowl/.

a no-show on the Monday after the big game, so what? As a manager I had a new point of view. I looked at the group and thought, "Oh no, my mortgage depends on whether the Broncos win or lose?" Part of my paycheck depended on these people showing up on Monday morning in "good health," starting the week off right. I only wish I were viewing the world through a momentum lens versus my default inspiration lens. I may have come up with ways to keep those day-after-Mondays from interfering with momentum!

Dealing With Financial Issues

Let's talk about some strategies for dealing with financial issues. When I work with managers, especially sales managers, we focus on the idea of recruiting bench strength, even if there are no open positions, to get more from the salesforce. The idea is, it is easier to demand behavior if there is a replacement on the bench ready to step in if things don't get done. Bench strength makes it easier to build and maintain momentum.

We can apply this concept to financial momentum too.

When we have resources in reserve, or on-the-bench as I say, ready to deploy when needed, our risk profile changes. Everyone has their own risk tolerance level, and in sales, when we have assets in the bank, it's easier to build momentum.

Let me give you an example. At the time of this writing, most people have been made aware of the WeWork/Adam Neuman saga. WeWork is an office space leasing company. They were among the first to create a collaborative office space sharing system for small companies, freelance workers, and remote workforces. In the go–go days of the late 2010s their charismatic leader, Adam Neuman, made headlines for his bold vision of a new way of work based on his experience growing up on a commune. As he sold his vision to investors, employees, and customers, his sales grew and competitors moved into the space.

Independent of WeWork was an ambitious investor named Mayoshi Son who headed up the successful Softbank Vision Fund. Son was working on a theory that if a startup in a wide open space had more funding they might be able to take out all the competition and own market share because they had access to more money than their competitors. This isn't news. What is news is Son thought, what if the company didn't just have more money, but had 30–40–50 or even 100 times more money than their competitors? They'd almost be guaranteed to win.

When Mayoshi Son met Adam Neuman, it was the meeting of two people with unusually high appetites for risk pretending they could build the ultimate financial bench to fund their dreams. With nothing to hold you back, what would you do?[4]

They had comparatively unlimited capital to deploy as needed compared to their competitors.

If you know the story you know how it ended up. It turns out that limits may be a good thing but it helps illustrate my point. When you have reserves you can take bold action. And in the case of Adam Neuman, he acted on it. I've used Adam Neuman's pitch to Mayoshi Son as an example of preparation meeting opportunity in sales. If Adam were your sales rep, he not only comes to you with outsized confidence, but he's got enough financial backing to take an already high-risk profile and turn reckless.

WeWork's funding is an extreme example, but it holds even in the low stakes worlds I am working in. I have observed the power of financial bench strength, both abundance and poverty, on the behavior of reps.

Imagine two reps, alike in every way except financial bench strength. Both have missed quota for a couple of months and are in do-or-die quota situations. One has an emergency fund equivalent to six months personal expenses in her checking account, and the other is operating paycheck to paycheck with no savings. Neither one wants to get fired from their job, and they're both at risk. Imagine them sitting in front of a demanding prospect in a heated sales negotiation when the buyer does something inappropriate. The buyers ask for a kickback on the sales reps commission to get the sale. In this example, kickbacks are not only inappropriate, they're illegal.

Both reps need the sale to hit goal and keep their jobs. This buyer has created a mini crisis in their brains as they consider the consequences.

---

[4] *The New York Times*. February 17, 2018. "The WeWork Manifesto: First, Office Space. Next, the World." www.nytimes.com/2018/02/17/business/the-wework-manifesto-first-office-space-next-the-world.html.

What happens next? If they say no, can they live with the consequences? If they say yes?

I've been in similar situations. The more desperate we feel, the more likely we are to compromise our ethics and justify risky decisions. Risky actions are a momentum killer.

This is why we tell our reps it's to their advantage to build a strong financial bench, have a full tank of gas, keep your powder dry, and a bunch of other related sayings. We want to keep feelings of desperation away. When we feel like we're out of options, we are.

As a manager it's almost impossible, and probably not appropriate, to know your people's exact financial situation. However, you can talk about the benefits of money in the bank for activity. Especially when coupling it with easier subjects like the benefits of a good night's sleep, eating well, and exercise. Financial bench strength keeps activity going. It helps your people make the right decisions and gives them the patience to stick to process, regardless of short-term pressures.

The takeaway? Promote financial bench strength. It helps.

Dealing With Health Issues

Health issues, like financial issues, can be devastating to momentum. In general, when addressing health issues it helps to think of them in two categories.

Known health issues
Future health issues

With known health issues the goal is to remove them. They are the bands holding you back from getting the momentum you're after. Whether it's something cosmetic like not liking what you see in the mirror, or it's something internal like chronic back pain, the solution is the same.

Small steps add up over time.

Momentum doesn't come in a rush. As a matter of fact, the most impressive momentum takes the longest time to build. Since removing a restraint is just as effective as pushing ahead, we can look at our existing health issues as obstacles to be overcome bit by bit, day by day. There is a simple tool to help with this, one that game makers have known forever and technology companies build regularly into their products.

Tracking your streak.

You've seen this and may even use it yourself from time to time. A visual representation of a streak helps us make small steps every day. Whether it's something like Jerry Seinfeld's advice to a comedian who wants to improve his joke writing to get a wall calendar and make a red X on every day he writes a joke, or seeing fictional character Andy Dufresne chip away at his cellblock at Shawshank every day, when we track a streak we start to build momentum.

For existing health issues, we overcome them by acknowledging their existence, then acknowledge every time we do our best to overcome them. Tracking it visually is what gives it power and drives momentum.

This is different than what we do with future health issues.

The nature of future health issues is we don't know when they'll come or how severe they'll be. It's unknown.

Like my friend who has just been diagnosed with cancer. One day she is out walking, going to the restaurant with her daughters, and a week later, she is reviewing a battery of tests with her doctor and making a choice about treatments. You can't streak-track your way out of that one.

What you can do is take a strategy and planning approach to future health issues. You know you'll have to deal with them at some point, whether it's your health or the health of a loved one. Not only do you know you have to deal with health issues in the future, you have probably dealt with them in the past. Whether it was a common cold or something more severe like work stoppage due to a torn Achilles tendon.

Things have happened and you dealt with them.

You know what? Things will happen again.

In my strategy work we call this kind of planning "preventative action" planning. Since we know some things have happened in the past and can imagine them happening again, we can take actions to make sure we're ready in case they do to minimize the event's impact on momentum. This may be as simple as not using 100 percent of your paid time off, always keeping a week in reserve, or keeping regular instructions for your co-workers on what to do in case of your absence. These preventative actions, it has been said, are worth far more than the actions we take once something happens. "An ounce of prevention is worth a pound of cure."

Wimbledon is a tennis tournament in England known for its insistence on tennis players wearing white, strawberries and cream, and its lush green grass courts. What's less known about them is their excellent preventative action planning.

Wimbledon is held over three weeks each summer and relies on massive television contracts and healthy attendance to exist. If the tournament can't take place, the impact on the community is devastating. Long before March 2020, Wimbledon took preventative action on events that might interrupt their tournament. They took out insurance policies.[5] The chance of a large interruption would have been miniscule in 2003, but they could imagine it, had dealt with stoppages before, and were ready in case such a thing happened. Like a pandemic in 2020.

You can help yourself and help your people maintain momentum by taking time to think through what has happened to you health-wise and consider it happening again. Preventative actions can be put in place to keep the momentum going. Like regular health checkups for instance.

Which brings us to the other part of health issues. What about the things you don't know, like my friend with her cancer diagnosis? (Caught in time, thank goodness! She is healthy due to early detection via a regular health checkup. Visit the doctor!) When you don't know what's going to happen, how you can plan for it?

You can't!

What you can do is put contingent actions in place. If preventative actions are what we put in place knowing something has a chance of happening, contingent actions are little processes what we put in place in case the unknown happens.

When it comes to salespeople's health, I think it's best to approach it like we might with financial issues. If the best time to get to know a banker is when you don't need one, the best time for a producer to get close to a doctor is before they need them.

---

[5] C. Ruel. n.d. "Wimbledon Set for Coronavirus Windfall in Huge Pay-Out From Pandemic Insurance," *Insurance Times*. www.insurancetimes.co.uk/news/ wimbledon-set-for-coronavirus-windfall-in-huge-pay-out-from-pandemic- insurance/1433146.article.

Just this morning, as I write this chapter, I am fresh from a doctor appointment. It's a checkup with a doctor I don't see very often, and don't have much of a relationship with. He asks two questions and gets to work. The last time we saw one another was nearly six years ago. He's a dermatologist, and once I tell him I'm only there for a checkup, he starts. A quick scan of my upper body and face. Nothing on my legs, feet, or other part of my body. I don't know if it's a normal checkup procedure or not.

Contrast this with my regular doctor who I see once a year. He starts every appointment with a review of our past appointments. If I brought up an issue in the past, he asks about it before I tell him why I'm there. "How's your back? Your left knee? Your allergies?" At this point, we've been doing this dance for more than a decade. We have a nice relationship.

If I have something happen to my health, even if it's a skin issue, where will I turn? Exactly. The doctor I have the relationship with. I think I'll get better advice, or at least a specific referral recommendation that comes with background. This goes for dentists, chiropractors, or anyone we rely on for health advice. In the United States, most citizens have a relationship with health care that relies more on Google searches than expert diagnoses. When something happens and the typical U.S. patient visits a physician, not knowing their patient's well-being puts the doctor at a disadvantage. Therefore, to keep momentum going, it's a good contingency practice to build relationships with physicians. If you don't have a relationship now, a good question to ask when looking for a referral is "Do you have a physician you would make sure to update if you were traveling and diagnosed with a health issue?" If they say something like no, or not really, keep looking. A good physician relationship should be as important as having a good banker relationship because your future momentum may depend on it.

When it comes to momentum, exercising discipline in your finances and health go a long way toward keeping you in motion. Take it seriously.

Good Stuff in Chapter 3

- Discipline issues are those that depend on checking a box a day, setting good habits.
- For Momentum we look at two types of Discipline issues: Financial and Health. Both are known momentum killers.

- Keep your finances in check with "financial bench strength." You make better decisions with a stronger bench.
- Keep your health in check with both Preventative and Contingent actions. Have paid time off (PTO) available for emergencies, and do regular doctor visits.
- Stopping a bad behavior is just as powerful as starting a new one. Try both when shoring up these momentum killers.

CHAPTER 4

You're Not a Robot— Intellect and Emotions

Overview

Intellect and emotion are what makes us uniquely human. Our humanity encourages momentum or takes it away. In this chapter, we cover ideas around keeping emotions in control and how to use intellect to our advantage in "respecting the streak."

It's time for the next segment of the wheel, our Humanity Elements, Figure 4.1. The two areas we're going to get into are Emotions and Intellect, the things robots can't get to yet.

Figure 4.1 Humanity in the momentum flywheel

Dealing With Reality: Blake and Don

At some point in your selling career, you've bumped into the characters you see in Figure 4.2, Blake and Don Draper. Blake is a character in the movie "*Glengarry Glenn Ross*," played by Alec Baldwin. Don Draper is a character in the TV show "*Mad Men*," played by Jon Hamm.

Let's start with Blake. He's polished, he's poised, he's successful, probably smells great, and he's been sent by Mitch and Murray to fix a broken sales team. When you first meet Blake, he is all business.

Blake: They all here?

Williamson: All but one. Ricky Roma.

Blake: I'm going anyway. Let's talk about something important … you're fired. The bad news is … you've got, all of you've got just one week to regain your jobs starting with tonight. Starting with tonight's sit. Oh? Have I got your attention now? Good. 'Cause we're adding a little something to this month's sales contest. As you all know, first prize is a Cadillac El Dorado. Anyone wanna see second prize? Second prize is a set of steak knives. Third prize is you're fired. Get the picture? You laughing now?[1]

It's classic boiler room sales banter. The play came out roughly 40 years ago, in 1983. The movie premiered 30 years ago. Yet even now, clips of Blake are making their way around sales offices worldwide.

Figure 4.2 Blake and Don Draper

---

[1] J. Foley, dir. and D. Mamet. 1992. "Screenplay," *Glengarry Glen Ross*.

A lot of sales managers and trainers have Blake in mind when they deliver motivational tidbits to their teams.

Here's the thing: Blake isn't real. The character was added to the movie by author David Mamet at the request of the studio to add tension to the movie. Like so many works of fiction it is a distilled version of humanity. Blake is all business, all the time, 100 percent focused on his task and doesn't have time for anything like emotions or the messy business of living.

He is built as the bad guy, the unseen force offstage that propels the action in the movie. His appearance is less than five minutes long, yet he steals the movie. So why is he a model for salespeople worldwide? I'll let Blake tell you.

Blake: "I made $970,000 in commission last year, how much did you make?"

Keep in mind this is in year 1992 dollars. It's like he's saying "I made $2.04 million in commission last year." The idea of being that focused and that successful drives a lot of salespeople.

If Blake represents the lack of Emotion in humans, Don Draper represents Intellect. The ability to deliver the perfect pitch at the perfect time to win the big deal.

Let's listen to Don delivering the perfect pitch to Kodak about selling their new slide projector. He's in a conference room and Kodak has given the ad agency the ultimate challenge in selling their newest invention, the photo slide wheel. They want the ads to include the "wheel" as they call it. A wheel is old, but their technology is new. What is Don to do?

> **Don:** "… My first job I was in-house for a fur company working with an old pro copy writer. . . He said the most important idea in advertising is 'new'. . . But he also talked about a deeper bond to a product. Nostalgia."
>
> (The room darkens as Don flips through photos of his family.)
>
> "[he] told me that in Greek, nostalgia means literally, 'the pain from an old wound.' It's a twinge in your heart, it's more powerful than memory alone. This is not a spaceship. It's a time machine."
>
> (Don goes through the slides in reverse order.)
>
> "And it takes us to a place we ache to go again. It's not called 'The Wheel,' it's called "The Carousel."

(The slide show ends with a slide of Don and his wife kissing, then a blank screen. An executive overcome with emotion, holding back tears, runs out of the room.)[2]

Impressive to read. More impressive when delivered by a skilled actor like Jon Hamm. But not real. The reason we love fiction is because the stories have elements of truth in them. In this chapter, we're going to talk about the way these two elements of our Humanity encourage or impede Momentum.

Being Human, Emotions: Keeping Emotions in Check

Emotion and sales go hand in hand. Salespeople know emotion drives action. The emotion of a threat (Blake) or the emotion of desire (Don Draper) spurs people into action.

In the Momentum Wheel, I am not referring to the emotion we use in sales presentations. I am thinking about our internal emotional state, and specifically how we handle emotions. It's a trendy topic in the United States today, especially Silicon Valley, where a lot of business trends originate; there is a fascination with Stoicism. An ancient Greek and Roman philosophy that teaches us to keep emotions in check. It's used as a sort of manual for the high achievement set and its core tenet is that if you can't keep your emotions in check, you can't be effective. Or, to put it another way, by keeping your emotions in check you will be more effective.[3]

We won't get into Stoicism but we will pick up on this point. If you can't keep your emotions in check, Momentum is at risk.

I have worked with some extremely talented salespeople and some of the most talented people were held back by one thing: their inability

---

[2] M. Weiner. 2007. *Mad Men*, Season 1, Episode 13, eds. M. Weiner and R. Veith.
[3] "…being able to implement emotion regulation strategies in the laboratory is closely linked to well-being and financial success." S. Côté, A. Gyurak, and R. W. Levenson. 2010. "The Ability to Regulate Emotion Is Associated With Greater Well-Being, Income, and Socioeconomic Status," *Emotion* 10, no. 6, pp. 923–933. https://doi.org/10.1037/a0021156.

to control their emotions. An extreme example is a young man I worked with who had a diagnosed psychological disorder. He was subject to extreme mood swings. When he was in a euphoric state, there was literally no better salesperson in the city. His enthusiasm was infectious. Successful selling depends on the transfer of emotion, and when my friend was on a high he transferred this emotion with ease.

The problem with my friend's high moods was they were followed by his low moods. He would swing from the most productive salesperson on the team one month to not showing up for work for days. His inability to control his emotions took him in and out of action, wreaking havoc on his momentum. He needed serious professional help and got it. When I think of emotions and its effect on momentum, he comes to mind.

It isn't just about moderating emotions. Part of emotional control is using emotion to drive momentum, which brings NBA Hall of Famer Michael Jordan to mind. In the documentary *The Last Dance*, Jordan's success is recounted through interviews and footage. In one exchange, after having won three championships he recalled an event that helped him channel emotion to win the 1996 contest between the Bulls and Supersonics. This anecdote happened during the championship round.

> Jordan's friend Ahmad Rashad tells a story about Jordan and Rashad at a restaurant. SuperSonics coach George Karl was there, too, and as he left he walked by Jordan's table without saying hello.
>
> Rashad remembers thinking to himself, "Uh-oh, shouldn't have done that."
>
> Jordan remembered thinking, "Oh, so that's how you're going to play it."
>
> Karl and Jordan both went to North Carolina, saw each other in the summer and golfed together.
>
> "That's a crock of (expletive)," Jordan said. "That's all I needed for him to do that, and it became personal."

Jordan controlled his emotion to create action and enhance momentum. He harnessed this minor, perceived slight into anger and used that to elevate his play, accelerate his momentum, and win a fourth title.

Emotions can help you build momentum. Emotions can lead to stopping momentum. The trick is to be aware of them.

Being Human, Intellect: Never Stop Learning

The second part of our Humanity affecting momentum is our Intellect. Intellect is the ability to grasp new concepts and draw threads between new information and past experiences. To frame this part of ourselves, it's best to learn from a couple of heavyweight organizational psychologists, Danny Kahneman and Carol Dweck. Kahneman is a Nobel Prize winner and, for much of his early career, worked with Amos Tversky on thinking about thinking. These two were fascinated by how we think, the shortcuts our brains take to get us through life. My few sentences won't do it justice, so I encourage you to pick up "Thinking Fast and Slow," and go deep into their work. For our purposes let's jump into one idea as it relates to intellect: System 1 and System 2 thinking.[4]

Put simply, our brain processes information in two ways, fast and slow (see Figure 4.3). The business of thinking takes so much energy, we have developed a high-level brain processing system they call "System 1." This way our brain processes information to make quick judgments and

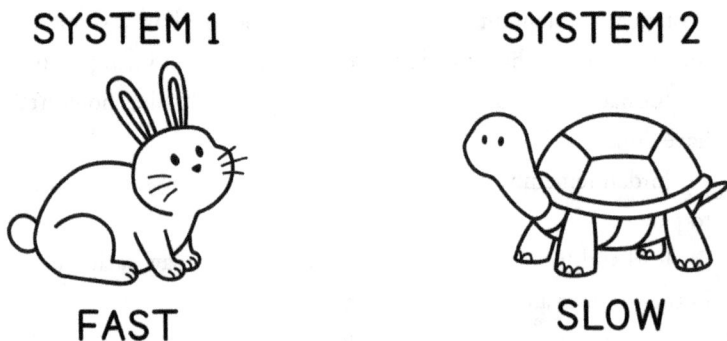

SYSTEM 1

FAST

SYSTEM 2

SLOW

Figure 4.3 System 1 and System 2 thinking

---

[4] D. Kahneman. 2011. *Thinking, Fast and Slow* (New York, NY: Farrar, Straus and Giroux), pp. 19–30.

move on. In sales we're pretty good at taking advantage of these heuristics, or decision-making shortcuts, to help prospects make decisions. For instance, some common heuristics are "if it's expensive it's good," "if a doctor endorses it it's good," or "if I said it, I must mean it," and so on. These shortcuts may be accurate 100 percent of the time, but they get us through life. If we had to think hard about everything, every day, we'd never get out of bed. Slower System 2 thinking, on the other hand, is our deep-thinking analytical brain at work. We reserve System 2 thinking for difficult problem solving. As an example of how Systems 1 and 2 thinking works, imagine we're standing in front of the cereal aisle in a typical U.S. grocery store. System 2 wants to take every box down from the shelf and inspect the label. System 1 thinks, "honey bee good," picks the Honey-Nut Cheerios box, puts it in the cart, and moves on. Keep these systems in mind for a minute, while we meet Carol Dweck.

Carol Dweck's contribution to our momentum lens is the idea we have a particular mindset about learning. Her idea has been debated in the Organizational Psychology world, but it works for us because she uses two buckets too. Her buckets are a fixed mindset or growth mindset (see Figure 4.4).[5]

Her argument is we are either prone to thinking humans are stuck with whatever brainpower and intellect we have (fixed) or we think humans can continually add more intellectual capacity (growth). For instance, when it comes to the capacity to pick up a new language, a fixed mindset says, "Greg, you're 50, if you haven't picked it by up now, you won't," while a growth mindset says, "Greg, keep at it! You're never too old to learn new tricks."

Just as System 1 and System 2 aren't good or bad, fixed and growth mindsets are what they are. As they relate to the building, maintaining, or recovery of momentum, it's important to have these buckets in mind because our momentum depends a lot on how we talk to ourselves.

Momentum and confidence go hand in hand. Like motivation and momentum, confidence and momentum exist together and apart. Without confidence it's hard for momentum to do its magic. With confidence

---

[5] C.S. Dweck. 2016. *Mindset* (New York, NY: Ballantine Books Trade Paperback), pp. 32–45.

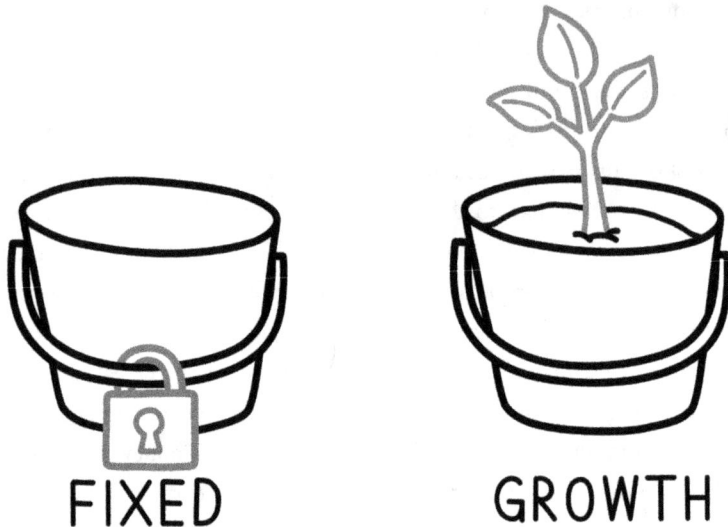

Figure 4.4 Fixed and growth mindsets

our momentum carries us further than momentum alone can take us. Confidence is all about our self-talk.

I met a young woman in college and knew her to be an attractive, healthy midwestern girl. Over the course of a year she lost a lot of weight. She wasn't a big woman, but she became obsessed with being too big. Seriously obsessed. After a year abroad, she came back to school looking much frailer than before. I don't know if it's correct to say she developed anorexia or became anorexic, but by the time we started fall semester her clothes were barely hanging on. By spring semester her parents had her committed to a local health care facility to nurse her back to health. I tell you her story because of something I experienced when visiting her in the hospital. During my visit, she walked me through her treatment and one part of her treatment that sticks with me was her patient diary. The doctor asked the patients to keep a journal of their thoughts. It was kept in a steno pad, which is a half-letter page-sized notebook having ruled lines and, most important to know, a dividing line down the middle of the notebook (yep, stenography was still a thing in the 1990s). Her instructions were to record her inner thoughts in the following fashion: on the left side of the pad go your positive thoughts, and on the right side write down your negative thoughts. She desperately wanted to be out of the hospital and as she explained this part of her treatment, I thought to myself, "Simple. You're a smart girl. They want to see you thinking positive thoughts, so give them what they want. Fill up the left side of the notebook, leave the right side empty."

When she flipped through the pages of her notebook, there was page after page of teeny-tiny, perfect script, with almost no spaces. The script was only on the right side of the notebook (see Figure 4.5). It was sad to see a mental illness illustrated so clearly, and the idea of her inner voice never thinking a single positive thought about herself jars me to this day.

Our momentum, the ability to build it, sustain it, or recover it, is influenced by our self-talk. Intellect, for momentum's sake, is the ability

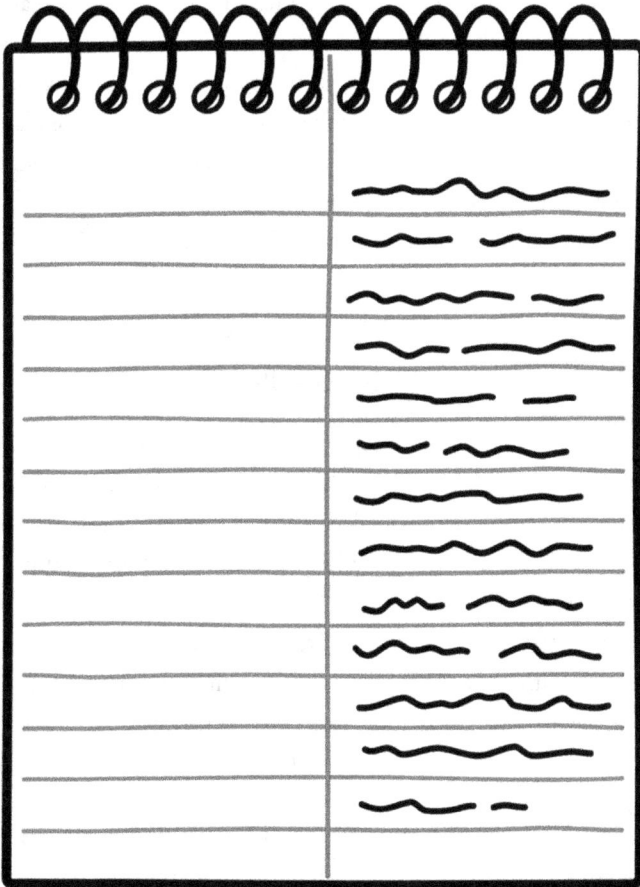

Figure 4.5 Steno pad thoughts

to think about how we think. "Meta cognition" as they say. When we can catch ourselves taking mental shortcuts (System 1), we need to force ourselves to take the time to think deeply on a problem (System 2). When we recognize ourselves putting up an artificial boundary (Fixed mindset), and can turn it into being expansive or generous with our boundaries (Growth Mindset) we can build momentum. If this meta cognition does not take place and our thoughts are out of our control, like a small boat being thrown about a stormy ocean, our momentum is interrupted.

Just like controlling our emotions (or at least trying to control) helps with momentum, controlling our intellect (or trying) helps with momentum.

When I work with clients on these ideas, the conversations can get a little dicey because when someone exhibits a lack of emotional control or lack of intellectual rigor, they require professional help. This is not just with the extremes of behavior like my bipolar and anorexic friends. I just use them as examples. I'm just saying, if you're dealing with extremes, get trained, professional help.

Warnings aside, let's get into what we can do with Emotion and Intellect.

Dealing With Intellect Issues

My wife, the community college professor, likes a quote attributed to the Greek philosopher Plutarch, "The mind is not a vessel to be filled, but a fire to be kindled." This ancient framing is the best way to approach our thinking about intellect as it relates to momentum. Never stop learning.

For "never stop learning" to take place we need something that may seem antithetical to our striving for momentum and progress. We need down time. Specifically, we need to sacrifice our efficiency to make room for learning. We need to fill this space with a bias toward learning.

For many of the people I work with there is some element of forced learning that takes place during their workweek. Whether it's breakout sessions in a trade show, informal lunch-and-learn trainings, or official continuing education (CE) credits required by their licensing bodies, those are good but not what I'm referring to here. I'm not even talking about learning things that are directly related to your profession. I'm talking about making time to grab any new level of knowledge or expertise in anything that interests you.

As children we did nothing but try and learn new things. Whether it was a sport like soccer, or sitting in a field with a Field Guide trying to learn the names and markings of wildlife, when you're young you are naturally inclined to have a bias toward learning.

At some point this leaves us. After raising my family and watching my kids go through school, I think the nature of our formal education system has something to do with this. The education system is designed to produce experts for the benefit of society and it does a good job of that. It also teaches us that amateurism isn't something to aspire to. We're encouraged to be a professional, be the best, or don't bother. Those are our unspoken metrics. In order to build momentum, we need to be more flexible in our thinking, and one way to do that is to embrace amateurism and pick up new skills.

It may be too late to be a child prodigy, but you can learn a new skill. Robots are programmed to do tasks, but humans can pick up new skills at any time. Over the pandemic, for example, I started to learn more about gardening. The "right plant, right place" ideals espoused by the gardening professionals have yet to yield results, but digging in the dirt is fun. Each time I do it and one of my plants survives I think to myself, "Yes! Take that robots!"

Let's take a minute to give ourselves a structure around how to go about learning a new skill from my friend Dan Rehal, CEO of pharmaceutical communications company, Vision2Voice, based in Chicago, Illinois. Dan explained adult learning this way (see Figure 4.6):

- Take in new information (Tell)
- Internalize it (Show)
- Apply it (Do)
- Teach it/Own it (Review)

TELL

SHOW

REVIEW

DO

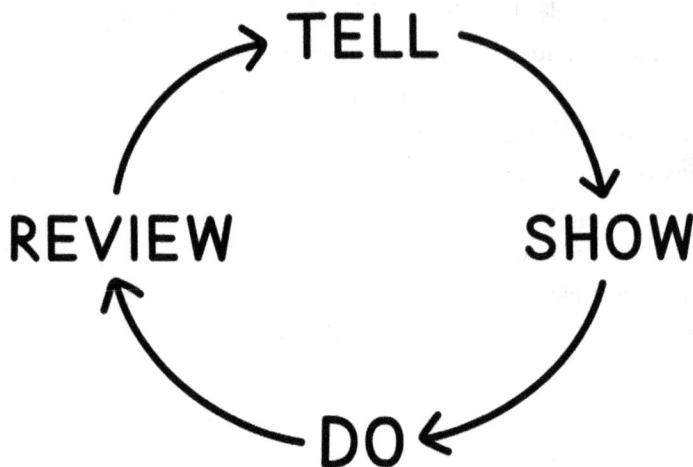

ADULT LEARNING

Figure 4.6 Adult learning cycle

The last step is the highest level of learning. When you pick up a new skill and try to describe it or teach it to another, you're practicing your bias toward learning. You're being human. You're building momentum. Tell, show, do, review. It's how adults learn.

Dealing With Emotional Issues

What about Emotions? What can we do to control and direct our emotions to keep them from robbing us of momentum, and instead, encourage momentum? This may sound like a digression, but stick with me here. The way to think about controlling emotions is by thinking about information.

The modern world is a firehose of information. By wading into this flow of stories and data, we are subtly being influenced by what we see. The information we consume impacts our emotions. When I bring this up with clients, they think my advice is going to be, "unplug." It's not. I am not going to advise turning the flow of information off, ignore the news, or limit your intake to inspirational platitudes. I want you to be an informed citizen. That said, be aware, not beware, but be aware of the motivations behind the information coming at you. It's not anything to be scared of, but when information comes your way it is not neutral. I find it easiest to think about information this way: someone has a job to do. Whether it's human or a robot, they, like most of us, are assigned a task. They are just doing their jobs to the best of their ability. The good people at Lexus want me to buy a car. Every bit of information they push into the river of sounds, words, and images I consume is doing its best to get me into a Lexus.

There is nothing wrong with that.

To get my attention in this flow, they have to stand out in some way. If everyone is saying and thinking X, they need to bring attention to Y. Most of the information we get is pretty mainstream. If it were in a normal distribution, most everything we see, hear, or read falls into that mainstream middle. To stand out, we need to get to the fringes.

You may ask why I'm on this tangent in talking about emotions. I'll tell you.

The easiest way to get your attention is to say something contrarian to the mainstream. If everyone thinks the French are favored to win the World Cup, I am getting no traction with the world if I say the same thing. However, I can get attention for my message if I say something contrary, like "The top 5 reasons France will lose in Group play."

Putting this into the world will get me noticed by serious soccer fans in France because it will make them angry. It's a ridiculous take, but the more I double down in my assertations and push my reasoning, the angrier their fans will get and the more recognizable I will be. Anger is our strongest emotion. It's easy to manipulate. Just ask any married couple about what they do to "press the other's button."

This is what I'm getting at. To control your emotions, question information. Insert a "pause."

There was a sales training I attended years ago, and the trainer was telling us we needed to develop a Pause. He said the world is giving us Stimulus, every hour, every day. We're going to Respond to this Stimulus. It's either going to be an automatic reflex or something a little more deliberate. His example is a house cat. The cat is all Stimulus/Response. You stomp the floor unexpectedly (Stimulus) the cat jumps (Response) and runs away. There is no Pause in a cat's world.

Humans, on the other hand, can develop a Pause. We can train ourselves to temper our Responses. We can learn to take a moment and think about the source of the noise, then consider our Response.

To control Emotions, consider the Pause. Before getting outraged, consider the source of the material and the job they are trying to do. In holiday ads I see the big bow on top of the Lexus at Christmas, the beautiful woman's surprise, and immediate expression of love to her gift-giver. When I think to myself, "I want that." This is when I need to pause. I need to ask myself, where is this information coming from? What is their job? Now, what's my reaction?

How to get good at the pause is a book of its own but I can offer one bit of advice from current research.

Sleep

This coming decade you'll see a lot of emphasis on getting enough sleep.[6] When it comes to regulating emotions, to being able to insert a Pause in your world of Stimulus, sleep is your friend. The researchers will tell you it's because your prefrontal cortex regulates emotions. This is where the energy for a good "pause" builds and is stored. When we sleep, we recharge. When we don't sleep, it's harder to pause. A parent only has to look at their experience with babies to confirm this. Even if you don't have kids but maybe have a pet, you'll know the adage "It's best to let sleeping dogs lie."

Without a well-rested prefrontal cortex, the monkey parts of our brain control us. You may have heard the monkey brain analogy, but just in case, it's the idea that the primitive parts of our brain are descended from the advanced parts of the brains of monkeys. Our amygdala, as it's called, regulates our fight-or-flight response. Very helpful in nature. Monkeys use their amygdala a lot. They are all stimulus/response. When we humans and our big human brains are not well rested, we are much more likely to be all stimulus/response, driven by our amygdala. We are much more likely to feel anxious. Or excited.

---

[6] M.P. Walker. 2021. "Sleep Essentialism," Brain 144, no. 3, pp. 697–699. https://doi.org/10.1093/brain/awab026.

So, get your sleep.

Along with getting sleep, we have another way to regulate emotions. We can name or label them. When you put a label on how you're feeling, something happens. "I'm feeling unusually anxious today" said out loud does something remarkable in our bodies. This is from the book "*The Upward Spiral*" by Alex Korb, PhD (emphasis added by me).

> … in one fMRI study, appropriately titled "Putting Feelings into Words" participants viewed pictures of people with emotional facial expressions. Predictably, each participant's amygdala activated to the emotions in the picture. But when *they were asked to name the emotion*, the ventrolateral prefrontal cortex activated and reduced the emotional amygdala reactivity. In other words, consciously recognizing the emotions reduced their impact.

Getting sleep and naming your emotions are effective tools to maintain high levels of activity.

Awareness Is the First Step

This chapter reminds us it's good to be human and our human elements drive momentum, but they might also rob us of momentum. Getting "on a roll" is harder when we battle limiting thoughts or negative emotions.

This chapter is one that can come off a little "woo-woo" or touchy feely, but this is only because our emotions and intellect are so strongly correlated to Being Human. As the Dude in the Big Lebowski might say, "They're inside you, man." To talk about emotional control or to force ourselves to take a few minutes to try something new, which we'll be bad at, is hard. It's contradictory to our tendency to push through and ignore our more fragile humanity. It's hard to fight the urge to be a Blake or a Don.

I'll leave this subject with one more memory. Years ago, I was the adult responsible for taking my grade-school-aged kids to an event at a roller-skating rink. I am not good at roller skating, barely knew the parents of the other kids, and reluctantly settled in for an evening of watching the clock while keeping an eye on my kids.

As I watch, I see another dad, Dr. Prabhu, on the rink, desperately clinging to the wall. The man is a genius, but it is obviously his first time on roller skates. "Knucklehead," I think. "You're a brain surgeon for goodness sake!" His kids are filled with delight as they zoom around slapping him on the legs when they speed by.

He is having the time of his life.

This is one of those moments my inner thoughts interfered with my momentum. Not sales momentum, but family momentum. I knew intellectually I didn't want to skate and fall. I knew emotionally I didn't want to be embarrassed. And I also knew Dr. Prabhu was having a ball, and my kids would love to see me out wobbling around.

Stimulus, Pause, Response.

After my pause, I took a deep breath, grabbed some skates, and slowly made my way around the rink. This time it's my kids zipping around, grabbing at my hands, and slapping the back of my thighs as they zip by. Everyone enjoying my amateur struggles.

It's good to be human.

Good Stuff in Chapter 4

- Humanity issues are those that deal with our responses to outside stimuli.
- For momentum we look at two types of humanity issues: emotional and intellectual. Both can enhance our momentum, and both can be obstacles.
- Keep your emotions in check by managing information intake and getting a good night's sleep.
- Keep your intellect in check by thinking about thinking. The stimuli is going to keep coming but it's up to us what we do with it.
- Awareness of emotions and intellect is the second step in harnessing a sales momentum mindset. With your humanity in check, it's easier to respect the streak.

CHAPTER 5

Give It Up to Get It— Support Systems and Belief in a Higher Power

Overview

Building and keeping momentum in a complex world is hard. When we acknowledge our dependence on support systems and surrender to belief in a higher power, it helps momentum. In this chapter, we cover ways to enhance your support system and tools for fighting the idea of "deserve" to stay in motion.

YNWA

We're not walking through life alone. There is a myth in sales of the swashbuckling entrepreneurial type riding alone in the frontier, sourcing new business, and conquering new markets, the Pale Rider of business development. It's not true.

When I started in life insurance sales, I was encouraged to work with older and wiser salespeople. The price for collaborating with these elders was to share my commission check. This was explained to me as the fastest way to learn, but it seemed silly. Why would I give up a percentage of my earnings to some old guy who didn't have to do the hard work? These opportunities were my relationships, my "lay-downs," my bluebirds.

Looking back, it makes sense. Sure, I built my own momentum in the early days, months, and years, but ran into trouble midway through year two. My progress came to a halt as I struggled with a few hairy situations with clients. Looking back, a grizzled veteran may have been able to help me navigate the situation. A veteran with a financial incentive to help me may have pushed me through the obstacles and helped my momentum, because my lay-downs and blue birds were anything but easy sales.

With these experiences in mind I want to talk about the next two elements affecting our personal momentum, Support Systems and Belief in a Higher Power (see Figure 5.1).

I titled this subchapter YNWA. Those of you who are professional soccer fans may recognize it right away. It's the acronym for "You'll Never Walk Alone," the Liverpool football club's anthem. Modern music fans may have heard newer versions of the song. The reason I'm bringing it up is because of this lyric:

> Walk on, walk on;
> With hope in your heart;
> And you'll never walk alone;
> You'll never walk alone.

Figure 5.1 Surrender in the momentum flywheel

When it comes to keeping momentum, it helps to know you're not walking alone. You're not riding solo on the edge of civilization fighting for survival. It will be easier to build and maintain momentum when you have a strong support system, and belief in something bigger than yourself, like a higher power.

Surrendering: Higher Powers

Let's start with the element closest to sounding like one of the third rails of things you don't talk about. "Don't fall into the trap of talking religion or politics," advised Mr. Carl. For selling situations it may make sense, but for building momentum it pays to look at our capacity to believe in a higher power and what happens when we don't.

Let's start with this: beliefs govern behavior.[1] This is true when advising companies about company culture (my day job) and it's true when we look at our own actions day to day. But where do these beliefs come from? It's easy to think behaviors follow beliefs but in most cases it's the other way around. Author Kurt Vonnegut said, "We are what we pretend to be, so we must be careful about what we pretend to be." This examination of our beliefs and the existence of beliefs of powers outside our control, Higher Powers, greases the skids of momentum.

Don't just take me at my word for it, philosophers and poets have been examining beliefs in higher powers for eons. For instance, let's look at what poet, musician, artist Nick Cave has to say about it. Nick Cave is the lead singer of the music group, "Nick Cave and the Bad Seeds," among other talents. This is from his question-and-answer letters with fans, Nick Cave's Red-Hand files #55.

This need to believe in something beyond ourselves is a basic human function ... this is not simply wishful thinking or lack of

---

[1] I. McGregor, A. Tran, E. Auger, E. Britton, J. Hayes, A. Elnakouri, E. Eftekhari, K. Sharpinskyi, O.A. Arbiv, and K. Nash. September 2022. "Higher Power Dynamics: How Meaning Search and Self-Transcendence Inspire Approach Motivation and Magnanimity," *Journal of Experimental Social Psychology* 102, p. 104350. https://doi.org/10.1016/j.jesp.2022.104350.

nerve or being "stupid," but a survival instinct that can bring great meaning to our lives, whether or not it conforms to the facts.[2]

It's that last bit that sticks with me. Belief in a Higher Purpose is our human "survival instinct" in this uncertain world. We've already said that momentum depends on how we deal with the role of Fortuna, luck, and circumstance especially when it comes to hard work that goes unrewarded. This is a real thing we deal with every day. As I write this, my son is preparing to marry his long-time girlfriend. They've been engaged for over a year and both families are thrilled to see them start a life together. A few months ago, his future bride's mother was diagnosed with a fatal disease. No one knows for sure how long she has, we only know it's tragic. Bad luck. Terrible circumstance.

Things happen.

My son is in sales, I'm writing a book about momentum, so of course, we've talked about the obstacles ahead and his reactions to them (see Figure 5.2). We're not an outwardly religious family, but we do have a strong belief in a Higher Power. It's hard not to. From time with young

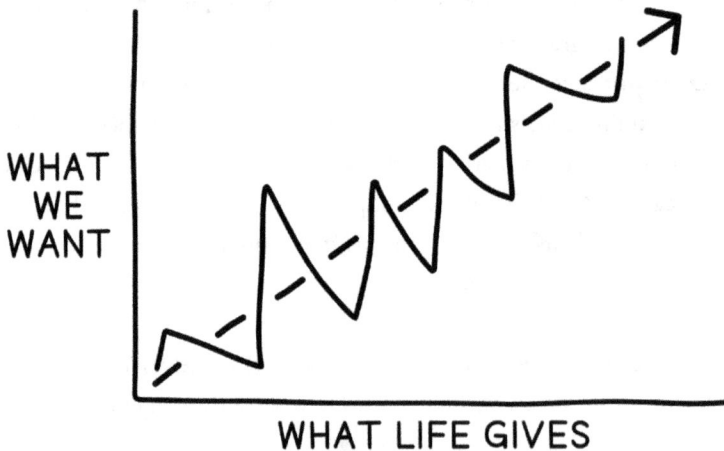

Figure 5.2 *The pull between what we want and what life gives*

---

2 N. Cave. August 14, 2019. "Nick Cave—The Red Hand Files—Issue #55—Do You Believe in Signs?" *The Red Hand Files*. www.theredhandfiles.com/do-you-believe-in-signs/.

kids spent looking at the sky's millions of stars, to contemplating the luxurious disappointment of losing an Internet connection in an important sales presentation. It's hard to escape the feeling that there is something out there, something bigger, influencing our momentum.

This doesn't mean we need to tilt toward superstition and reading the tea-leaves for signs. As Mr. Cave continues in his letter:

> Far be it from us to believe in signs; far be it from us to believe in spirits; far be it from us to intuit indications that the universe is not as it seems or, worse, that the dead are trying to tell us something—oh no!—because that would make us delusional (Richard Dawkins) or intellectually dishonest (Sam Harris) or in denial of death (Ernest Becker) or unreasonable (Steven Pinker) or cowardly (Bertrand Russell) or stupid (Ricky Gervais) … and we can't have that! Yet here we are, with these lurking suspicions, these hunches, all around us. (Cave 2019)

I am not here to judge your particular Belief in a Higher Power. I've run into all kinds of beliefs over the years. My first summer out of university, I struggled to find a job. My confidence is low, I have no momentum, but I need to make some money. I find an ad for a caterer who is hiring. I know nothing about the industry but a friend of a friend said working at weddings could sometimes lead to big tips. I met the owner and his wife, got a quick tour of the facility, met the chefs and wait staff, and was hired on the spot. Start tomorrow, they said.

My job is to deliver catered breakfasts and lunches to the large law, accounting, and consulting firms in downtown Denver, Colorado. My trainer is older than me by a few years and has been working for this family for a long time. We head out at 5 a.m. to deliver breakfasts and lunches, and he tells me to make my own lunch to bring along. I'm broke and I love to eat, so this is going well. Around noon, after we've picked up the trays from breakfast and dropped off all the box lunches, he tells me to grab my lunch. We're going to watch the Denver Grand Prix trial runs. Sounds great, I think. I could get used to this.

When we get back to the office around 4 p.m., my trainer jumps out of the van, heads toward his car, and yells over his shoulder some vague instructions about how to clean up. I walk into the facility and my new co-workers start whispering. I'm new to the job, but wise enough to know something is going wrong, and it's probably my fault.

The owners march me into their office and the beatdown begins. It turns out there isn't a free lunch, and there is never an excuse for not returning to base after a delivery, because with only a few trucks, there's always another job to deliver. Stop and watch a car race? Was I crazy?

My ex-co-worker is long gone. I'm left thinking this angry Italian (the owner grew up in Sicily, moving to Denver as an adult) is going to fire me at the very least, fire me and make me pay for his lost revenue at the most. I'm damp in the palms, sweat is running down my back, and I can barely speak.

Now, this isn't a story of *my* belief in a higher power. This, my friend, is about my new boss' belief in a higher power. His higher power, it turns out, is his fortune teller.

The next morning I arrive at 5 a.m. to receive my verdict. I can tell the staff is curious to see me come back, but they notice I'm carrying my newly issued logoed polo shirts too, so we all know what's going down. I walk in to face my executioner, and with a smile on his face, this nice man tells me a story. He hired me that first day on the spot because his fortune teller told him I would be coming in. When I blew my first day's work, this same fortune teller told him it was all part of the plan.

I not only kept my job, but I was also given a small raise, some added responsibilities, and expected to make an impact. Momentum won't be stopped today!

Whatever your belief system is, whether it's driven by behaviors or vice versa, it's powerful.

Surrendering: Support Systems

There's a debate raging in the press as I write this book. Working from home versus working in an office. Right alongside this debate are the Great Resignation and Silent Resignation discussions. The underlying thread with the career changers seems to be, should we be working as hard as we do, and if so, how should this work be structured?

By the time you read this the debate may be settled, but when it comes to momentum, the research tells us work is good,[3] whether it's remote or in person, especially from a psychological standpoint. It provides us with contacts and support.

In my book "*The Human Being's Guide to Business Growth*," I talk about work passion, telling managers it's the wrong thing to think about. For anyone in sales I give the same advice. Work is how we support ourselves, but your job doesn't need to be your passion. Your career is made up of the work you do throughout your life. You may be in sales, you may be in education, or business, or a creative pursuit, but a successful career doesn't need to be tied to your passion. Your career is the sum total of all the experiences you have doing all the work you do. It doesn't have to be a vocation.

This is what a momentum lens help us keep in mind. When we get away from motivation and focus on maintaining activity in our work, we get more done in less time. Part of building or keeping momentum depends on our Support Systems.[4] Do we have them and what do they tell us about the work we do?

In sales, we are solving big problems. From a high level we are taking what we know about our company's products and services and trying to help our prospects make the exact right decision for their company. We know that without problems to solve, our products and services are worthless (and if you don't know this, pay attention to this digression!).

The products and services we sell get their value from the problems our customers are trying to solve or the results they are trying to achieve. We sell more when we keep this front and center in our minds. Let me give you an example.

Imagine I show up at your office wheeling in a snowblower. It's not just any snowblower, I tell you, this one is powered by solar. Its advanced

[3] M. Csikszentmihalyi. 1990. *Flow: The Psychology of Optimal Experience* (New York, NY: Harper and Row), pp. 158–162.

[4] "...family relationships play a central role in shaping an individual's well-being across the life course." P.A. Thomas, H. Liu, and D. Umberson. 2017. "Family Relationships and Well-Being," *Innovation in Aging* 1, no. 3, pp. 1–11. https://doi.org/10.1093/geroni/igx025.

battery system holds a charge for months at a time, even on cloudy days. What this means to you, Mr. Prospect, is it will be ready to go when you are. No oil changes, no empty gas cans, just ready to go. It has enough power to handle anything up to a five-car extended driveway on a corner lot. This snowblower not only has power, but it can also handle everything from a three-foot snowdrift to a small dusting of snow. It won't just clear your driveway, it will clear sidewalks, flagstone paths, and make grass paths for little Fido to do his business by the back tree. It can even handle pea gravel porches without making a mess. The best part? It's a robot. With its advanced AI, satellite GPS, and your Wi-Fi connection, once you show it around the property, it's powerful brain senses the weather and operates independently, without any instruction from you, for the entire winter. It's pet safe, environmentally friendly, and has a setting to go looking for old people in a one-mile radius to help. The best scientific minds in the world have been working on this snow-blowing technology for decades. I can say to you in all honest, Mr. Prospect, this snowblower does everything.

The prospect nods his head, mouth slightly agape, not knowing what to say. The machine is beautiful yet slightly menacing. It's ready for work. Then the prospect smiles and says, "Greg, this is an amazing machine. But I live in a penthouse apartment in a high-rise. And we're in Phoenix."

No snow problem, no value. There is no inherent value in the machine. To find snow problems, I need to get out of Phoenix and make my way to Houghton, Michigan, where the annual snowfall is 218 inches.

What does this have to do with passion? Or support systems? You know what you have to do to make sales. Passion for your solution helps, but passion for uncovering your prospects, problems, or desires is the most important behavior you need to exhibit. This brings your Support System into play.

If your Support System believes in your ability to uncover problems to match prospects to their exact right solution, you'll build momentum.

On the other hand, if your Support System thinks your career should mirror your passions and hobbies, or hates your product, company, or boss, your momentum is at risk.

Support Systems should help you focus on behaviors, not results. Sales is all about sticking to a process, one that is ideally focused on uncovering a customer's value, and if your Support System, whether it's family, friends, co-workers, or an Internet chat group, is behind helping you execute your work behaviors to the best of your ability, that builds momentum.

Dealing With Higher Powers: The Goddess Fortuna (Again)

What can we do to enhance our Belief in a Higher Purpose? It's a good question, and to help with the answer I want to revisit our goddess Fortuna again. Acknowledging luck in all its forms is where we can start recognizing there is something out there for us that's bigger than today's selling activities. It gives us some perspective. We're going to work to the best of our abilities, of course, but we need some good things to happen to us along the way.

If you've ever listened to the podcast "How I Built This with Guy Raz," with Guy Raz, you'll know he loves to ask his guests a question near the end of the interview. He asks whether luck or hard work accounts for their success. Here is what one of the cofounders of Instagram, Kevin Systrom, said:

Luck is a big part, but you have to recognize it, have the talent to take advantage of it, and then do the work.[5]

The luck for Instagram was the combination of apps on our phones; photos, filters, social media, and big networks. They weren't the first with any of these things. They weren't the best funded, and weren't the smartest but they persisted. Recognizing the role of luck and attributing it to something bigger than you helps you build momentum. As you make progress, be aware. As Systrom went on to say, "I have this thesis that the world runs on luck. Everyone gets lucky for some amount in their life. And the question is, are you alert enough to know you're being lucky or you're becoming lucky?"

[5] G. Raz. n.d. *Instagram: Kevin Systrom & Mike Krieger: How I Built This With Guy Raz*. NPR.org. www.npr.org/2018/01/02/562887933/instagram-kevin-systrom-mike-krieger.

I interpret that as Belief in a Higher Power and love how he grounds it in work. Things that happen are a mystery, he seems to say, so are you going to just let it happen to you or are you going to try and put it to work day in and day out. As Ben Franklin, founding father of the United States of America, puts it:

Energy and persistence conquer all things

He that can have patience, can have what he will

Human felicity is produced not as much by great pieces of good fortune that seldom happen as by little advantages that happen every day

Considering Fortuna, acknowledging luck, or putting our results in the hands of a Higher Power, all build momentum. The opposite: expecting hard work to pay off by itself, chokes momentum off. Start building up your Belief in a Higher Power by getting to know Fortuna.

Dealing With Support Systems:
Who Do You Lean on?

There is a popular saying among the achiever set that you become the average of who you hang around. I don't disagree with this notion, but if we take this thought to heart, we may end ditching friends and family, which might not do much for building a Support System that encourages Momentum. This is why we need a way to get more from our existing support systems (see Figure 5.3) instead of recreating one.

Figure 5.3 Looking for behavior feedback

An acquaintance of mine confides some of his darkest fears to me. I'm one of his few outlets because unlike his family, employees, and investors, I don't depend on him for anything. From the outside in, this is a person with an amazing support system. He cultivated this group by working with some of the best minds in finance before family obligations brought him back to Omaha. Today, he helps run one of our largest companies and is a pillar of the community. His "average of who he hangs around" suggests a stellar support system.

What are his dark fears, you ask? Those are less interesting than where his fears come from. His dark fears have their roots in his Support System. The way they give him feedback results in his momentum being stymied, as often as it is stimulated by this group. We talked about why this happens, and over time we teased out why it takes more than just being surrounded by ambition and achievement for your Support System to help with momentum.

The lesson we can take from this high-powered executive is that the rank and privilege of a support system is less important than the style feedback they give you. Inside your own Support System then, it makes sense to teach your supporters how to help you, regardless of their stations in life. The best way to do this is to train them. Approach their support, especially their feedback, as you might train a dog. If you've ever been involved in training a dog, you know what I'm alluding to. You can't really make a dog do anything. What you can do it recognize a behavior you want and reward it. Want to teach Fido to shake? As you say "Fido, shake," over and over with one hand extended and a treat in the other hand, wait for him to randomly reach out and touch your extended hand. When he does, "Fido, shake!" you exclaim, "Good boy!" and hand over a treat. Rinse and repeat until Fido puts it together. "Fido, shake" means put a paw in your hand and let you do a goofy handshake for a treat.

A Support System needs the same training. You can't expect them to know what you need to build momentum, so it's on you to recognize when they are commenting, good or bad, on your actions versus your results. You want to applaud or tsk-tsk your behavior, not your outcomes. You can train your support system to recognize your best behaviors, and ignore outcomes.

After learning this from my high-powered friend, I see it happening all the time. It turns out, you can train even the most Type-A, nononsense achiever to give feedback on behaviors. You can even train the slackers in your orbit too. It's up to you to recognize behavior versus outcome feedback and react accordingly. The good news is humans are more intuitive than dogs and we learn quickly to give you more of what you react positively to, less of what you fight against. The hardest part for us when we train our people is not reacting poorly when feedback on a behavior is negative. It's much easier to control reactions to comments on your good behavior. My advice? When receiving feedback ask yourself if they are talking about your behavior or an outcome. If it's an outcome, a result, or a consequence, ignore it. However, if it's a behavior, action, or attitude (good or bad), smile. Thank them. Insert your Pause in the Stimulus–Pause–Response sequence when you're getting feedback. It's hard to do if the negative feedback is about a poor behavior, but long term it's what you need.

The language we use for all feedback is, "Thank you. That's right."

We specifically use the word "that" because research has shown that when we say "*You're* right" to feedback, our brain does its best to keep the input at arm's length.[6] The "you" in "you're" isn't you, yourself. It's them. It's their problem. Saying "you're right" keeps the feedback from sticking with you. However, when we substitute "that" for "you're," we are giving credence to the feedback itself. Our brains will acknowledge the feedback as valid and our subconscious will go to work incorporating the feedback into our behaviors.

Your Support System is important for Momentum, but it's just a part of what you need to build speed. Whether you are born into privilege or working your way out of poverty, having an effective Support System is in your control. A trained support system can be used to your advantage and build Momentum.

Now is the time for you to say, "That's right," to yourself.

---

[6] C. Voss. 2017. *Never Split the Difference: Negotiating As If Your Life Depended on It*, (London: Random House Business Book), pp. 105–107.

Good Stuff in Chapter 5

- Surrendering elements are those issues relating to how we walk through this world interacting with others and with Fortuna.
- For momentum we identify two surrendering elements: higher powers and support systems. Both can enhance or stifle momentum.
- To acknowledge a higher power is to admit that life is complex and you're doing your best. Hard work is the price to pay in sales, but it's not always rewarded in our expected timeframe. Sloth, on the other hand, is not rewarded.
- Build your support system by encouraging the right kind of feedback. Ignore outcome-related feedback like, "great commission check!" and encourage behavior-related feedback like, "You worked so hard for that. Good job."
- The opposite of working with surrendering elements is to approach life with a sense of entitlement. When we take thoughts of "deserving" out of our way, momentum builds.

CHAPTER 6

Navigation—Mentors and Hidden Rules

Overview

Staying in motion requires navigating obstacles. In this chapter, we cover two types of navigation: mentors and knowing hidden rules. Mentors are easy to find, but for momentum we need a particular type of advice. Hidden rules are harder to find, but through questions and mentors we can find them faster, preserving momentum.

"You Want to Get Out of Here? You Talk to Me."

One of my favorite movies in my teenage years was *"Mad Max."* The perfect blend of dystopian nightmare, nihilism, and hero's story.

In the movie, our hero, Mad Max, has, through a series of remarkable events, finds himself inside a fortress-like oil refinery. The refinery is surrounded by terrible people trying their best to get in, get the petrol, and lay waste to everyone inside. Max has spent a few years on the outside battling these mobile gangs for meager trappings in a postapocalyptic desert. The people in the refinery want to get away to a coastal paradise promised in some brochure, but to leave the refinery is to risk certain death. Their latest attempt at breaking through the bad people's blockade ended badly, pulling Max and his vehicle into the compound.

As the leadership debates their next steps, Max listens. He knows all too well what waits for them on the outside, and it's not good. As the trapped citizens come up with crazier and crazier plans, Max speaks up.

"You want to get out of here? You talk to me."

A perfect metaphor for the importance of our next topic, navigation (see Figure 6.1).

In this chapter, we're talking about the last of our four personal elements of Momentum. We've covered the following:

- Discipline Elements: Our Finances and Physical Well-Being
- Humanity Elements: Our Emotional Control and Intellectual Firepower
- Surrendering Elements: Our Support Systems and Belief in a Higher Power

Now we're going to delve into our Navigational Elements. Specifically, the presence and interaction with Role Models, and Knowing the Hidden Rules.

Figure 6.1 Navigation in the momentum flywheel

Navigating With Mentors: Who's Your Mentor?

Let's start with defining what I mean when I say Mentor. Part of my day-to-day work-life is spent Mentoring, Coaching, and Teaching (see Figure 6.2). Look them up in a thesaurus and you'll see all three of these words are interrelated, but I use them in a specific way.

- Teachers introduce new information to you and help you process and contextualize it for your own application. The transfer of this knowledge is their key function. They will describe it, they will show you how to do it, they will watch you do it, and listen to you explain it to others. They give information and it's up to you to make use of it.
- Coaches bring in outside evidence to help you reach a goal. You want to accomplish X. A coach observes your activities and gives you a different point of view, identifying gaps, reminding you of the target, and helping you get there. You must tell the coach where you want to go. They'll help you get there.

COACH

TEACHER

MENTOR

Figure 6.2 Coach, teacher, mentor

- Mentors, on the other hand, are responding to the input you give them, running it through their experiences, and making suggestions. They may teach a little, they may even want to know what your objective is, but their real value comes from their knowledge of the world you're working in.

Mentors are important because they have been there, done that. It's a very specific type of knowledge. It's firsthand and it's experiential. I think I should point out that their experience may not be correct or factual, but it took place. The information you get from teachers may or may not be experiential. This doesn't make it any better or worse than a mentor's advice. When it comes to building momentum, however, we're after other people's experiences.

This book is based on experiential learning. I have been there, done that with dozens of companies and hundreds of individuals. From what I see, focusing on momentum works better than focusing on inspiration to consistently meet and beat quota.

From what I've seen, you need mentors to build and keep momentum. You need people who have consciously built momentum, who have helped others build momentum, and ideally, have troubleshot it when momentum is lost, either regaining momentum or helping steer others back on track.

When working in one of my startups, Mad Gringo Apparel, I bumped into all three types of advisors in my journey to fund the dream. Through my time working at a bank I had exposure to a lot of people with experience providing money to startups. However, they had never actually secured money themselves. Their value in helping me build funding momentum was minimal. Good information, but nothing more.

In my professional life I met a couple professional fundraisers. One had the connections that promised me a successful fundraising experience. I slot him into the coach role because he was there to help facilitate conversations, which is helpful. He had never run a small startup, but he knew how to get checks from investors. If the raising of money was the only objective it may have been a good solution to use him as a coach, but I needed more than just money to start.

In the end, I found a mentor through asking people for someone who not only had money to invest, but also had that money because they built a successful startup using investors. It's funny, when you're clear about what you're looking for and why, opportunities open. Being clear on what I wanted, led me to a good mentor who introduced me to other mentors. I would share my activity and he'd respond, directing me this way and that, telling me about experiences where he was successful or failed. This insight is what built momentum. It wasn't a roadmap to what I needed, but the mentor helped me see around corners and stay a step ahead of myself. "Watch out for this," or "Stay away from this kind of deal structure," were the words of wisdom I needed to build momentum, raise funds, and get more funding down the road.

Mentors and momentum go together. Know what you're looking for.

Navigating Hidden Rules: Culture and Hidden Rules

Part of what mentors can provide but separate from what you should expect from your mentors, is knowledge of a sales culture and hidden rules. If you've worked for more than one company over time this will sound obvious, but even if you've only been at one company this should be helpful.

Knowing the difference between what a company says they do and what they actually do has an effect on our momentum.

Let's define hidden rules and then define what I mean by culture. Hidden rules are any unspoken customs, practices, or behaviors that are not posted, published, or known except to insiders. I'll give you a couple of examples. In-N-Out Burger and Foreign Languages. Have you ever been to an In-N-Out Burger? The brand has been expanding eastward in the United States, but for a long time it was strictly a West Coast phenomenon. Living in the Midwest, I would hear people debate the best burgers and Californians usually offered In-N-Out as their entry into the contest. I traveled to California for business for a few years and the first stop I made on my first trip was to this venerated fast food joint.

It wasn't all that great.

I did the drive through and the menu is, well, simple. There's nothing to it. Burger, cheeseburger, fries are all I remember seeing. It came out in a paper tray and I sat in the parking lot thinking, huh, this is it? Must be a nostalgia thing.

On another trip one of my sales reps said we should grab In-N-Out. Whatever, I thought, and we got in line. When it came time to order my passenger said, "I want a cannibal, hold the mayo, drown the fries, and mix it up," or something like that. The nice young man taking our order didn't miss a beat and looked at me for my order. "Same" I said.

It wasn't the same burger I had the first time. It wasn't the same experience at all. One bite and I understood why In-N-Out was in the conversation. On my first visit, I didn't know the hidden rules. All I saw was a basic menu. I didn't know everyone customized their burgers and there was an entire language around which burger is what.

I just had to ask.

Foreign language is the same way for me. Even when it's English, my native tongue! I'm thinking specifically of an experience coaching youth basketball at the local recreation center. The kids on my team were from various economic backgrounds, (one showed up to practice wearing jeans!) and all of them spoke in slang and colloquialisms far different from what I know. I would explain things to them, listen to their responses, and think, what just happened? We tried, but game time would come and their relatives would scream instructions foreign to me, and most of the time, foreign to the players. It is like everyone needed translators. I had my knowledge of the hidden rules from growing up with organized basketball in the suburbs, but this group were learning a different game from the one experienced by me and my peers. Before my team could hope to build momentum, we would need to learn the basics of what we were trying to communicate. In my book "*The Human Being's Guide to Business Growth*," I used the image of icebergs to communicate this concept (see Figure 6.3).

On the surface are our words and actions, but underneath the surface is a world of experiences, many of which aren't shared. Getting this overlap is what linguists call a common underlying proficiency (CUP).

In "The Human Being's Guide to Business Growth," I used CUP to talk about defining terms. Here I'm using it to say that without working on the CUP, momentum stalls. It's too easy to think you understand something but miss the real message when CUP is low.

ICEBERG EFFECT

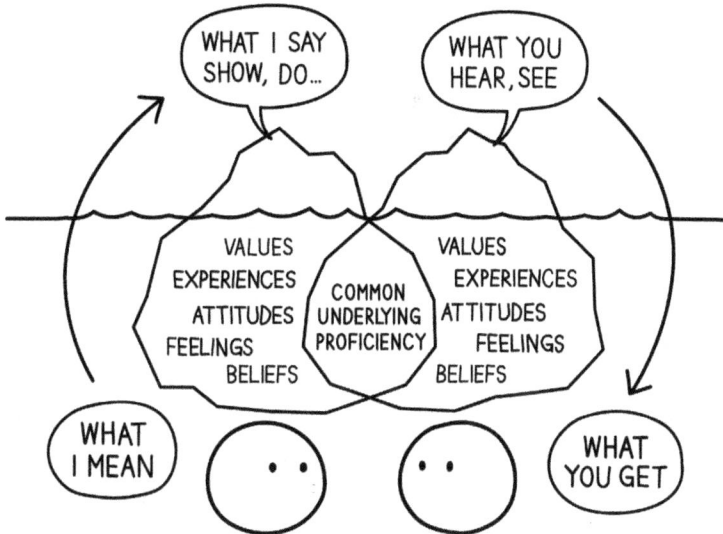

Figure 6.3 The iceberg effect of language

Knowledge of hidden rules either keeps the momentum going or can stop you in your tracks.

When you're inside an organization, we bundle these hidden rules into the word culture. Culture is the set of behaviors governing work inside the organization. For example, company policy may state you have two weeks of vacation to use every year. Company culture makes sure no one takes more than two days off at a time.

The challenge we have with hidden rules and culture when it comes to momentum is they are, by their very nature, not visible. We learn them through osmosis. Once I knew there was a hidden menu making In-N-Out the best burger place on the planet, I could ask friends and even family, "What do you get at In-N-Out?" It's like a world opened up because it did. Starbucks too (although I'm still thrown off by the names of the sizes).

For us to get momentum going, or keep momentum going, we need to know about our company's sales culture and understand their hidden rules. We also need to know our prospect's buying culture and their hidden rules. We need to find this hidden world of rules and behaviors to thrive. The good news is, there are ways to get it done.

Dealing With Mentors:
Role Models in a Pinch

Companies have mentor programs. Associations have mentor programs. Schools, churches, and volunteer organizations have mentor programs. It's important enough that everyone is trying to structure it for you. The problem with that approach, or plugging into a preset program, is that when it comes to your momentum, and sales momentum specifically, you need something very specific.

Since salespeople run into so many different situations, it helps if you can make developing role models in the service of your momentum, easy. Career mentors may come along once in a lifetime, but momentum mentors can be created whenever you need them. This is because we're looking for one thing: someone to help you see around the next corner.

That's it. You want someone with enough experience when you explain what you're doing now and they can tell you what they'd expect to happen next.

If it sounds simple it's because it is.

Simple doesn't mean easy, however. When you find someone with experience and describe your situation, they will give you advice in one of two flavors.

Top down or ground level.

A trait particular to our human species is we can draw maps.[1] This is good because maps are what you need to see around corners. The challenge with maps is some are going to be a top-down view, and some are a ground-level view, depending on who is describing it.

The good news is you need, and will use, both descriptions. Learn to recognize them by the words your mentors use when you ask for advice.

Top-down sales advice sounds like, "You need to know more about the players involved. Who is the economic buyer? Who is the strategic buyer? Who owns the business case? Who stands to win and who stands to lose?" It's almost like the mentor is staring down at a chessboard.

---

[1] B. Tversky. 2019. "Mind in Motion: How Action Shapes Thought," *Basic Books*, pp. 71–83.

Ground-level advice sounds like:

You know what you need to ask? Say, "describe the company's decision-making process to me." If they hesitate or get stuck, help them. Say, "other companies, about your size, for a decision in this dollar range, have steps like Gather Information, Check Competitors, Decide on the Business Case, Allocate budget …

It's almost like the mentor is imagining themselves in the conversation.

You need both these points of view. And the amazing thing is, you can get maps from anyone with experience, whether or not they have an official Mentor title. The trick is to recognize when someone speaks top-down, follow up by asking for ground-level examples, and vice versa. They're human so they can flip between the two points of view with ease. You just need to ask.

Start with "I need your help. What do you think is happening? What do you think I should do?" Listen, make notes, then ask yourself, "Does this sound more like a top-down map/chessboard? Or is my new mentor slipping into a role and giving me a script?" Then ask for the other version. Try it. It works.

Dealing With Hidden Rules:
Get the Part, Play the Part

For accessing hidden rules, my advice is less straightforward. The nature of hidden rules is they are not in plain sight. They aren't written down. And for many sales and buying cultures, the people involved have never tried to label the rules. It's like the old joke about the goldfish.

Two young goldfish are hanging out in the pond when one of the grizzled old goldfish of the pond swims by.

"Good day, boys. How's the water?" he says, chuckling to himself.

Once the old goldfish is out of sight, the boys turn to each other and say, "What's water?"

The hidden rules are like the water to the fish. We're surrounded by them, but if we don't get it pointed out to us it's like they don't exist. Makes sense; it's probably why they're hidden rules.

How do we crack the codes? The same way we make sales.

Ask questions.

In Season 3 of Michael Lewis's podcast, "Break All the Rules," he interviews a successful entrepreneur.[2] This guy says he is successful because he looks for, and finds, people who know the hidden rules. He takes their knowledge and builds software around it.

These aren't little ideas he's dealing with. The example Lewis highlights is the medical billing software company the entrepreneur built his fortune with, Athenahealth. He knew the system was complicated, he knew if he could make it simpler there was money to be made, he just didn't know how exactly he was going to do it.

As he investigated the market, he kept hearing a reference to a woman who knew everything about medical billing. She was a clerk and made it her business to know medical billing codes. She wasn't a high-level executive, she just moved from hospital to hospital fixing their billing processes.

They met, he tapped her brain for the hidden rules, got his programming guru to code her knowledge and sold this software to hospitals and medical clinics. The software was so successful at tapping her knowledge of the hidden rules, an unusual customer came calling. The health insurance companies! Yes, the makers of the rules were interested in his company's software because it knew more about how things worked than they did.

That's the power of finding and naming hidden rules.

Get there the same way as the entrepreneur did. By asking questions. What, How, and Why will get you furthest in this quest. What are you doing? How is it done? Why are you doing it that way? Get you close to the hidden rules. I've found that simply thinking, "What are the hidden rules in this place?" is all it takes to get started. When a salesperson starts at a new company, I tell them to start by looking for the hidden rules of their workplace. For instance, be wary of existing salespeople who want to be your friend on day one. In general, the most productive salespeople on the team are the least interested in making new friends because

---

[2] "Against the Rules Podcast," Season Three, Episode 1: Six Levels Down.

they're busy making sales. You want to be a top performer, so be wary of the overtly friendly team members and become a keen observer of the top performers. Once you start looking, you'll find hidden rules everywhere. Being aware is the first step to putting the momentum sherpas to work for you. The Sherpa people are a Tibetian ethnic group native to the Himalayan Mountain range between Tibet and Nepal. Some Sherpas are known for their excellent mountaineering skills and help lead explorations of mountains like Mt. Everest. They not only have experience with the mountains, but they also know the hidden rules of mountain climbers and the local community. They are both mentors and communicators. As you work on building sales momentum in your company, look for both a sales mentor and someone who knows the hidden rules in your organization. Pro tip: it helps to find people who know your prospect's hidden rules too. Your sales cycle speeds up faster than you think is possible.

Good Stuff in Chapter 6

- Navigational elements help us build and continue momentum by revealing obstacles in our path and helping us steer around them.
- For personal momentum we focus on two navigational elements: Mentors and Hidden Rules. Not seeing obstacles before they happen will bring momentum to a halt.
- Finding mentors for momentum is as easy as asking for advice and listening for top-down or ground-level responses. Once you identify which one you're getting, ask for the other.
- A lovely thought from my friend Tara Wisdom, CFO of OrthoNebraska in Omaha: "I have visually had the feeling as an oldest child I was navigating life in a wheat field (the western Nebraska farm town girl in me) pushing down the wheat as my sister easily came behind—forging her own path once in a while—yet knowing there was an easier one I already created. Leading in a way that gives a team the stability there is a path and support while letting them see/ knowing the goal creates a team going in the same direction and teamwork. I have been most successful as I have

navigated my career when given autonomy by those clearing the way for that success. Also knowing by clearing the path someone may pass you and being OK with that—takes time in your career to see—but the most successful people are training their replacement.

- Finding the hidden rules is harder. You get there two ways. First is through questions, asking What? How? and Why? about how things get done. Second is by observation, seeing the gap between what the company says and what the company does.

- For most of us in sales, finding mentors and learning hidden rules are fun. They make the job fun. However, our momentum can suffer without them. Get curious. Ask questions.

PART 3

Organizational Momentum—
Outside of You

Figure P3.1 Momentum flywheel and aqueduct

CHAPTER 7

Where Are We Going?— Clear Company Vision

Overview

This chapter marks the change from an internal focus, or things we can control, to external elements that are harder to control. The chapter looks at what a clear company Vision does to momentum. The clearer the destination and reasons for getting there are to you, the easier it is to stay in motion, building momentum.

We're making a shift. Up to this point we've been talking about what we need to do as individuals to build or maintain momentum. We've been focused on balancing our flywheeled bicycle so it rolls smooth and can gain speed. We know that releasing tension is just as effective as pushing harder and we're ready to destroy quota.

As the saying goes, we've been focusing on the thumb, not the finger.

Now it's time to look where the finger is pointing (see Figure 7.1). What does the ground our bike is going to roll on look like? Part of building momentum is having a smooth track to run on. And while the very nature of a track is that we're not in control of it, we need to know some things about it in order to take advantage of momentum.

Let's look at the Momentum Wheel again, but this time we're going to put it on the ground.

This section is made up of four elements. Each is represented on the slope we're trying to build momentum on. These are parts of the company you're selling for. While you may not have direct control over the elements, by recognizing them you'll be able to subtly influence them over time. If you're an executive looking at this manuscript for ways your salespeople can be more productive, up to this point I've been looking inside

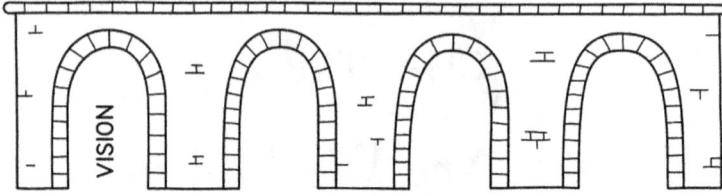

Figure 7.1 Vision in the momentum aqueduct

the salesperson. Now I'm going to dig into the company you're in charge of building. If you want your people to build momentum, get these four areas shaped up and smoothed over (see Figure 7.2).

The slope I've drawn looks flat, but really it's more like a Roman aqueduct than a flat surface. The ancient Roman aqueducts, some of which are still standing today, are marvels of architecture. As the Romans built their cities, they used aqueducts to transport water from sources miles away to the city centers. These water bridges are important to us because the Roman engineers built these miles-long structures at a slight slope for the water to run from the high point at the water source to the end point miles away. For example, the Aqua Marcia aqueduct built in 144 to 140 BCE moved water over 60 miles without pumps, using only gravity. It ran underground for about 57 miles, and then 6 miles above ground on substructures and arcades before it reached the city of Rome. Only gravity and a gentle slope. No pumps.

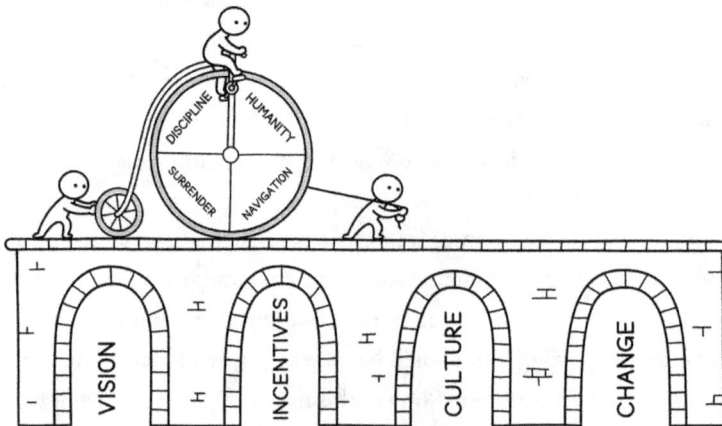

Figure 7.2 Momentum flywheel and aqueduct

No Motivation. Just Momentum

This is the kind of gradient you want roll on as a salesperson. You want an organization that helps you build momentum over miles and miles. Over months and months. The more momentum builds, the easier it will be for you to maintain that momentum and be inspired by Continuation motivation. When you're evaluating your company, look at these four elements of company momentum.

- Vision—where is the company going and why bother with the journey?
- Incentives—what do salespeople get as a reward for their effort?
- Culture—what are the behaviors and hidden rules governing the effort?
- Change—how resilient is the organization when changes happen?

Let's start with your company's Vision.

What Is Vision: Company Vision Communication

Mr. Carl, my old mentor making yet another appearance in this book, used to tell me, "Greg, every port looks good in storm."

You may see that and think, isn't it "any port in a storm?" and you'd be right. Mr. Carl was full of misattributed quotes and statistics, but this is probably why I remember so many things he said. Mr. Carl was saying, in his own way, that if you don't know where you're going and the storm hits, any safe place will do. He meant this derisively because in his mind when you know where you were going, storm or no storm, you're pickier with the port you choose.

What I take from his altered saying is this: your company's vision is important for your momentum as a sales rep.

The reason this is important to you is your company's vision dictates its strategy. Your company's vision and strategy dictate its immediate plans. And your company's vision, strategy, and immediate plans dictate the product mix, the commission plan, and the tools at your disposal for bringing on new business.

Important stuff.[1]

And not in your control. (The analogy of the finger and thumb again, see Figure 2.3. This one is the finger all the way.)

As a salesperson you want to know three things from your management team (see Figure 7.3). The company's vision is not technically in your control, but in order to act freely in pursuit of the same things your leadership team is after, your best bet is to get clarity from the top on these three questions.

1. What do you and the rest of leadership see happening in the world in, say, five to seven years? It is important to keep this question broad. If they ask for clarification like, "You mean in our industry?" tell them no, I need you to be broader than that. More like "What would be the world like in five to seven years?"

2. In the world at that time, what do you think our customers will be doing? This is where they should get a little more specific about your industry, but it's okay, even preferred, if they keep it broader than

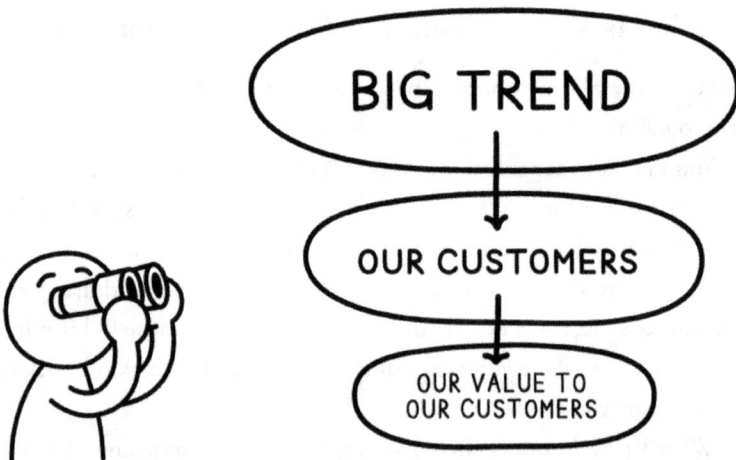

Figure 7.3 Describing the company's vision

---

[1] D. Maister. 2008. *Strategy and the Fat Smoker: Doing What's Obvious but Not Easy*, (Boston, MA: The Spangle Press), pp. 12–13 and pp. 233–235.

that. If question 1 is a worldview, question 2 is about how they see your customers operating in this world.

3. How do you see us, as a company, providing value to our customers at that time, in that world? This gets into how your company thinks they'll provide value to your customers at some point in the future. You can let your management get specific here, because the first two questions prepped them for this answer. This is the one you're really after. As you look down the aqueduct and plan your momentum journey, what do they think is going to be at the end of it.

As you might expect, there is no way to hold your leadership to these answers. You don't want to hold them to their word. Instead, treat their answers as you do with any predictions. Keep them in mind as you work because they point you in the right direction without being a specific destination. For Momentum to build, you need a direction much more than you need the destination. In other words, the revenue goal is less important than the idea of where the value driving the revenue is going to come from.

A client of mine launching a new product went through this exact exercise for his leadership team. Vikram Hegde has built a device for the world's largest hotel chains that helps their managers manage any connected device in their buildings. His answers are useful in learning what I think you should be listening for.

Sclera's new device tracks other devices. It's a complicated service, but for his intended market, hotel chains, it's a very valuable one. There's nothing worse than checking into a hotel and upon getting to your room finding out the Wi-Fi or the heating/air conditioning or the TV doesn't work. Vikram's team figured out a way to let the management team know what's working and what's not, minutes before the guest does, improving the customer's experience. We spent some time working through their vision, and once we worked the answers out, we used it for recruiting new team members, keeping the product development team on target, and even in our presentations to the giant hotel brands they are targeting. This is what we worked out:

For question 1 Sclera's leadership team will answer, "In the next five to seven years, the world will have more, not fewer, Internet of Things

(IoT) devices. McKinsey projects going from 1 billion devices cur-
rently to over 100 billion devices in this time."

For question 2 Sclera's leadership team will answer, "Knowing this, we
expect our customers to not only depend on more and more devices
to service their customers, we expect they will demand these devices
work better and are easier to use than ever before."

For question 3 Sclera's leadership team will answer, "To provide value
to our customers, our company will design solutions that make
using these devices to provide world-class customer service as easy
as glancing at a map. Making technology simple so *our* customers
can focus on *their* customers."

That's it. You see what I mean by it being too broad to be anything
more than a direction? Their sales team can listen for opportunities to
uncover value anytime they hear about a connected device malfunction
impacting a customer's experience. This is what you're after.

If you happened to sit through the lengthy Beatles documentary, "Let
It Be," at about one hour six minutes into the first episode, when the
Beatles have been messing around on their instruments for a while, Paul
says they need something to aim for. Otherwise they'll never be ready.
They come up with a day they'll have a concert and work toward it. From
that point on they are directed. They don't get to their original destination
in the timeframe they agreed on, but they get somewhere.

For you to build momentum you need to have a vision of where
things are going, just like Paul and the rest of the Beatles.

Using Vision: Alignment With Something

At this point you may be thinking, "Um, my managers won't have any
idea what I'm asking for when I ask about a vision." This shouldn't cause
panic, but it is concerning. Getting leadership and middle management
aligned on vision is a tough job. If there is no vision, there is only execution of a plan. The day-to-day execution of a plan is rarely enough to
build momentum on. The good news is, if you ask often enough you'll

probably get to the vision. The leadership doesn't know the script you're trying to uncover, so be patient.

What if you never get there? What do you do if you believe the vision isn't right? What do you do if the vision isn't exciting and you look around and think to yourself, "I'm not even sure I like these people?"

This happens. In my work I see the engaged salespeople, the ones who can build momentum and get to our goal of achieving Continuation motivation, as experiencing one of three kinds of buy-in to vision.

1. First, you may just buy into the vision. This is the easiest way to keep momentum building. They say we're going here, you say, I like that, and you get to work. Easy peasy.

2. If you don't buy into the vision, or can't get clear on the vision, I've seen salespeople succeed because they are bought into the customers. They want their customers to succeed so badly they can live with an unclear vision. I see this a lot in health care. The patients are so important to the salesperson selling into the space that they work through a muddled vision.

3. The last way I see salespeople build momentum with an unclear vision is they buy into their co-workers. It's not as crazy as it may sound. Many years ago, I read a Gallup survey on employee satisfaction at work and the #1 predictor of longevity was whether the respondent said they have a friend at work. If you like the people you work with, you give management a little more leeway.

Great, you say. I don't have any of these at my workplace. I'm 0 for 3.

Then you have a choice. A long time ago, someone described the law of the jungle to me. They said, "The law of the jungle is Adapt, Migrate, or Perish. Try, Fly, or Die." When you are faced with a workplace that can't describe their direction or you don't like the direction, you're indifferent about the customers, and you don't have friends you care about, I give you permission to resort to Jungle Law. Try to make it work by adapting. Or leave for another opportunity. Or accept your fate and know that every time you build momentum you're at risk of the aqueduct crumbling underneath you.

One More Thing: The Vision Isn't for Hitting

One last thing about vision. If your company does it right, and your managers have it right, you won't hit your vision. It should be always out of reach.

Why?

As legendary Nebraska football coach Dr. Tom Osborne was fond of saying, it's the journey, not the destination. When you can only chase the pot of gold at the end of the rainbow, an endless search you have no way of winning, you end up focusing on the regular business of day-to-day progress.

It's like what Amazon.com founder Jeff Bezos said about his company. "We are stubborn on vision. We are flexible on details."

For your sales momentum's sake, act the same way. Be stubborn on knowing where the vision is taking you but be flexible on how you'll get there. Keep your options open but keep moving forward. In this way, vision smooths the road for momentum to build.

Good Stuff in Chapter 7

- Our sales momentum is 100 percent dependent on us. Our environment has a lot to do with our ability to build or sustain momentum. There are four elements that help or hinder us. Company vision is one.
- Is your company vision clear on what they expect the world to look like? How their customers will act in this future world? How the company will provide value to those customers?
- If the vision is muddy, and you aren't excited about it, can you buy into your co-workers? Are you willing to do what it takes to overcome obstacles for the sake of your customers?
- If you have concerns about the direction of the company, Try, Fly, or Die. Either stay and figure it out or find the next place. If you sit there questioning, you'll die, killing momentum. Take action.

CHAPTER 8

What Do I Get When We Get There?— Sales Incentives

Overview

Salespeople and management agree on the importance of incentives, but both parties struggle with the static nature of comp plans. In this chapter we cover simple versus complex plans, and strategies for dealing with the inevitable need for plans to change.

Next up in our examination of what it is about the companies we work for that will make our sales momentum easier to build, easier to maintain and requiring less effort to regain, is every salesperson's favorite subject: sales incentives (see Figure 8.1).

When talking to people about incentives and their importance, one of my consultant friends said, "It's the best way I know for building momentum." TJ O'Brien probably wouldn't describe himself as a consultant because his career is hard to pin down. TJ is an accountant (CPA), a lawyer, became a partner at one of the Big 6 accounting firms, ended up managing a family office, and built a successful business around energy tax credits in the mid-2000s. In all of this work, he has taken a hands-off approach to managing and uses incentives as a way of motivating his direct reports.

TJ told me some of his success stories. Every success was built around setting up a generous payout or pay-split based on certain specific achievements. In the language of our last chapter, he set a clear vision, created a timeframe and destination to mark along the path to the vision, and created an incentive package to make the effort worth everyone's while.

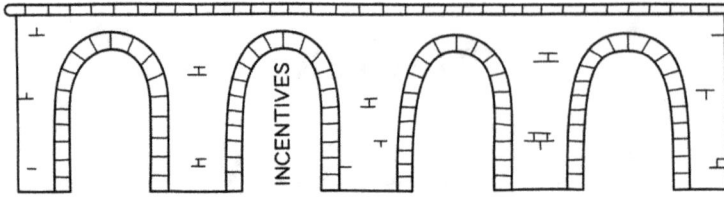

Figure 8.1 Incentives in the momentum aqueduct

His compensation plans are generous to the point where some of his partners question the necessity of the generosity, as in, "I don't think we need to be giving up that much, TJ." He'd stick to his guns. He knows that talking about goals and objectives is one thing, achieving them quite another. If he wants to be hands off and trust people to get where he and his partners want to go, the incentive, the payoff, needs to meet or exceed expectations.

It's in this spirit that we're going to talk about Incentives because for your personal sales momentum to build, incentives need to be two things.

1. Aligned with the company's objectives.
2. Workable in both short term and long term.

What TJ and the rest of us can agree on when it comes to incentives is this: the right incentives will undoubtably build and maintain momentum, but the wrong ones are guaranteed to kill it.

The studies tell us money isn't our main motivation for work. It may be true, but this is most likely to happen in a world where the incentives aren't aligned with what they want long term.

Thinking About Incentives

In our company's budgeting and planning process, the finance department has an outsized influence on what happens in the sales and marketing area of the business. This makes sense. If a business is supposed to make a profit for its shareholders, it needs a strong finance department to count what comes in and goes out, plus they need to project what's going to come in someday in the future, plus they need to make an accurate estimate of what future costs will be. It's this last estimate that we're most interested in, because some of those future costs include sales and marketing expenses, including incentives.

The problem I see is one others have described like this:

Often, sales team incentives and targets are only loosely connected to the profitability goals CFOs pursue. Connecting tech stacks, agreeing on shared KPIs, and creating common dashboards would help finance and sales move from finger-pointing to handshaking.[1]

Management types, skilled at seeing the world as income and expenses, know that one of the easiest ways to make sure they hit profit goals and earn their personal incentives is to manage expenses. Like managing salesperson compensation or bonuses or commissions. The thing is, as TJ O'Brien knows, if you can get your financial targets and sales incentives aligned, building the momentum required to achieve the company's goals almost takes care of itself.

Comp Plans: Simple Works, but So Does Complex

As a sales rep looking at your compensation/incentive plan, the tendency is to want something simple (see Figure 8.2). The challenge with simple is it rarely works for long periods of time. The exception to my rule (there are always exceptions) is in startup scenarios.

When you are in a startup, the challenge is to get noticed. The world has no idea who you are and this includes your prospective clients. To sell into this world requires an almost monk-like patience level because you're going to hear no. A lot.

Startups, to overcome this challenge, make use of flat rate commissions. These splits are often more generous than the compensation plans

---

[1] E. Wallace. March 30, 2021. "To Maximize Growth, Get Sales and Finance in Sync," *Harvard Business Review.* https://hbr.org/2021/03/to-maximize-growth-get-sales-and-finance-in-sync.

STARTUP

SIMPLE

ESTABLISHED

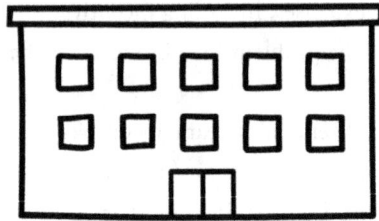

COMPLEX

Figure 8.2 Simple versus complex incentives

at more established businesses. The reason for this generosity is because you're going to earn it!

When I started my apparel company, Mad Gringo, I built a team of hired guns, independent sales representatives covering most of the United States. These veteran sellers ran their own manufacturers' sales teams and carried multiple lines of apparel. They were called "rag salesmen" because they traditionally carried bags of clothing to sell to retailers in their territories. Bags of rags. For a new line there is a competing set of motives for the rag seller. On one hand, they want to be the first one to carry a line in their territory to keep other salespeople at bay. Plus, if the line takes off and sells well, they want to reap the rewards. On the other hand, they aren't all that excited to take a new line out of their "bag" and make big claims because a new line that doesn't sell through may ruin a relationship. I loved hiring them because they worked on full commission, making it easy for me to cash flow, but since they were full commission I had very little influence on their selling behaviors.

Like I said, lots of competing motives.

My solution to make sure they took my "rags" out of their bags, and worked to overcome the objections their customers might have about this wisdom of taking a chance on a fledgling brand, was to incentivize them. At the time, an established but niche brand would pay a flat commission around 10 percent. If the product were selling well and the brand established, it may pay as little as 3 percent. For some brands each product had its own commission rate. For instance, a strong-selling basic white polo shirt is a staple kept in stock, so the minimum orders were high and commissions low. A high-end men's suit, on the other hand, has a more generous commission because these days suits are expensive to keep in stock and hard to sell.

To build momentum for my brand, I used a 25 percent flat rate commission for my incentive. I had to incent the sales reps to take my products out of their bags. If it didn't sell easily, I had to incent them to push a little harder to get me on the racks of their retailers. It wasn't a sustainable commission rate for the business, but it helped me alter the reps behaviors, and generated sales. If this kind of scenario describes the kind of product or service you are selling, a startup working to get market share, look for simple commission plans.

In a more established market your compensation plan should be more complex.[2] Established businesses have competing priorities, and the leadership teams spend a lot of time in meetings strategizing. You should expect the compensation plan to (a) be complex and (b) change frequently. This is a good thing for momentum if you know how to take advantage of it.

When your comp plan is complex and subject to change, spend a lot of your time learning the details of the plan. You should see every element of the comp plan and ask yourself, why would they make this choice? It's tempting to think your leadership team is a bunch of dolts making random choices in dark rooms, but that won't help you with momentum. "But, Greg," you say, "you don't understand how dumb the changes are." You're right, I don't. And I don't care. To build momentum you have to understand the vision, but you are not required to agree with the choices they make on how to get there. For momentum to build, your job is to come to a conclusion about why they are doing what they are doing. Do they want you to sell more of X? Less of X? Lock in longer contracts? Shorter payment terms?

Whatever it is the commission plan is asking for, to get momentum building you need to take advantage of it.

When I worked at a 150-year-old bank, we sold a 25-year-old service. The market was cutthroat and margins were tight. The team I inherited

---

[2] D. Chung. July 20, 2017. "How to Really Motivate Salespeople," *Harvard Business Review*. https://hbr.org/2015/04/how-to-really-motivate-salespeople.

were universally against the compensation plan leadership rolled out months prior to my arrival. "Why would they do this?" they said, and I said, "I don't know. I don't care. What I do care about is how you are going to maximize the plan they've given us."

It was not easy for these reps to push aside concerns about comp plans, but over time we made progress. The newest reps were the first to take advantage of the new structure. The veterans came around as they saw the newbies bring in impressive new commissions. Before I left that role the comp plan changed at least half-a-dozen times. Each time the group got better at managing their anger and keeping their momentum going. A common objection at each change would be, "If I start selling it a new way it's going to be bad for the customer." I never disagreed. But I knew it was probably only bad for some of the prospects they sold to. On the other hand, the changes were usually beneficial to other prospects. My job was to help them maximize their compensation in their new world. I'd ask, can we find customers it's good for? Can we uncover value in a new way? Is there some benefit we're not seeing yet? It was hard work for the reps to change their views, but we worked to keep their momentum going, and were rewarded for our flexibility. Again and again.

As I was leaving for a new position, one of the decade-old veterans of the job pulled me aside and said, "Greg, I've worked for a lot of managers. You're the only one that talks about maximizing incentives no matter what the change is, and I'll tell anyone who asks, I have made more money working with you than any job, ever." This was the same guy who told me in my first weeks on the job that the changes to his comp plan were immoral! He just needed to change the lens he was looking through.

Most people work in mature markets. Expect the comp plans to be complex and to change. Use it to your advantage for building or keeping momentum going.

One final takeaway on sales incentives. Some of them will be poorly designed and not thought through. Others will be masterpieces of corporate and customer alignment to a vision. Either way, the incentive plan is out of your control. How you react to it isn't. Remember the monkey brain? Stimulus–Response? You're not a monkey. Stimulus–Pause–Response. You can pause. You can choose the response. Don't let changes to the comp plan kill your momentum.

Good Stuff in Chapter 8

- Incentives in sales are important for momentum. A well-designed comp plan will stoke the engine of momentum; a poorly designed plan will bring the engine to a stop.
- A shortcut for evaluating comp plans is simple = startup, complex = established business. If a startup trying to claim market share has a complex plan, beware. If an established company has a simple comp plan, beware. Momentum may be a challenge.
- All comp plans change. Keep momentum going by taking time to dig deep to understand what the company wants and translate that into what's best for the customer. Being agile allows your sales momentum to thrive.

CHAPTER 9

What You Do, Not What You Say—Company Culture

Overview

Company culture, the shared set of behaviors inside of an organization, can either help momentum or stunt its growth. There are various tactics and techniques for figuring out a culture and using it to our advantage for building or maintaining momentum, tactics like minimum standards and data collection.

Is there anything more annoying than working with someone you know isn't trying?

From your momentum's perspective there is. When you put in less effort than normal because you look at an underperforming co-worker and think, "at least I'm not them" your momentum is affected.

This is the chapter I dig into company culture and its impact on your Momentum (see Figure 9.1).

Culture and Momentum: Best Player on the Worst Team

It's tough to be a superstar on a losing team. It takes extra effort.

I have another quote from another legendary football coach, Oklahoma's Barry Switzer. He is quoted as saying, "it's not the X's and O's, it's the Jimmys and Joes." It's not the plays and concepts, it's the players on the field. When you are surrounded by excellence, you raise your standards. Your Momentum depends on the soup you're swimming in. To pick up the example I used at the start, when you give less than 100 percent, for whatever reason, it's natural to take a look around. If others are putting in even less effort, or getting worse results, you take a breath and relax.

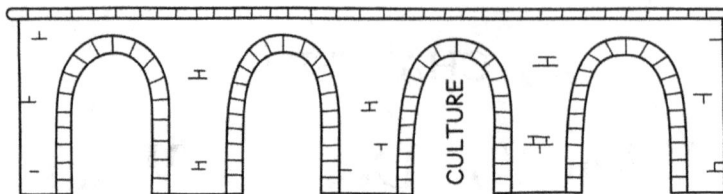

Figure 9.1 Culture in the momentum aqueduct

Bad for Momentum. Contrast that to when you look around and see others giving their full effort, maximizing results. You tend to give a little more effort. Good for Momentum.

I learned this from personal experience. I worked an inside sales job and used short-term Momentum to move myself into the top tier of performers. As I've mentioned before, when you focus on momentum it doesn't take long for results to show up. In this case, it was less than eight months into the new position before being promoted. I focused on what I could control, being there a little early, focusing on consistent activity, and it turns out, being relatively healthy and sober. At this time, a few years out of school, one of my college roommates was in a band. They were playing a concert in a city three hours away. On a Wednesday night, two other friends were driving down to see him and asked if I wanted to go along. I knew I'd be tired, but as a top performer with a few months of solid results behind me, I joined them. As you'd expect, we stayed late, had too much fun, and got back to town way later than I expected. They dropped me off, I took a quick nap, showered, and headed into the office. I felt horrible but did a passable job of being myself for the day. The worst thing that could happen to my momentum, happened. I closed a big deal and was praised for my performance.

It would have been better for my momentum if I had a horrible day, watched my rival salesmen set a record, and got yelled at. Instead, I went home thinking, "even at half-speed I'm better than the rest of these yokels," and my activity took a hit.

Company culture has been defined as the collective daily behaviors of its employees.[1] I'll take it a step further and say culture is the lowest

---

[1] A. Weiss. 1994. "Best-Laid Plans: Turning Strategy Into Action throughout Your Organization," *Las Brisas Research Press*, pp. 29–32.

common denominator more than anything else. The culture is a collection of the worst allowed behaviors in the workplace.

As an individual cog in a large machine you can't control your workplace culture, but you can manage its impact on your Momentum if you're thoughtful about it.

Changing Culture: The Culture of Momentum

The culture of Momentum in a company can start anywhere. It's best if the leadership is already modeling it, but it can come from the sales floor too. Get there by practicing a simple two-rule culture of individual momentum. Our first rule of individual momentum is don't ruin a co-worker's day. When you take this to heart, it allows you to make a particular demand. Part two of our two-rule momentum code is, if I make it a point of not ruining your day, I have earned the right to call out co-workers if they ruin mine.

Let me go a little further into this (see Figure 9.2).

When most of us get to the office, on a scale of 1 to 10, with 1 being angry at the world and 10 being full of joy, we show up somewhere in the middle. There isn't any reason to be pissed and there isn't a reason to be ecstatic. This changes as soon as we interact with others. In sales, long before you engage with customers you're going to engage with a co-worker or sales manager. If you come into the office at a 5, neither happy or sad, just ready to get some work done, and the first person you bump into is a salesperson complaining about how client services has screwed up another deal, as you listen you drift from a 5 to a 4. If the next

Figure 9.2 Don't ruin someone else's day

person you engage with is the resident grouch complaining about how there is never enough of the good coffee in the machine, you're now at a 3.

You haven't even started work yet, and momentum is at risk.

This is what I mean when I say your first rule is to consciously not be the someone who drags others down. When you consciously try to keep others level or even bring them up a notch with every interaction, and you do this consistently over time, you can practice rule #2. You have earned the right to demand the same courtesy from others.

When I used to onboard new employees in my organizations, I would tell the newbie we had a particular culture in place. This culture included many behaviors I was not aware of because I am so deep in my day-to-day activities that it requires an outsider to see them. They were the outsiders, and we'd slowly integrate them into our accepted and rejected behaviors. I'd say, if you've ever purchased a can of paint and watched the technician color it, you have an idea of how this works. The technician starts with a base of white paint. To reach the desired color, they start adding drops of color. One drop in a gallon may not do much, but two drops? Three? The gallon remains white until it reaches a tipping point when the last drop of color changes the paint into a new color.

Me and the company, I'd tell the new hire, we are the white base paint. They, the new employee, the outsider, are drops of color. Either they'll join our culture and blend into the white or the group will tint into a slightly new color.

With this simple "don't bring me down" rule, a single employee can change a culture. You can change the tint of your culture, regardless of how it exists today. Practice this first rule because you need to model the culture you want. Your Momentum depends on it. Demonstrate what respect for momentum building looks like.

Culture Challenges: High and Low Performers

As anyone who has spent time looking at a sales team's results can tell you, it's next to impossible to have everyone on the team be high performers. There will be a regular distribution of performances, and some will be off the charts high, others despairingly low. Believe it or not, no matter what the distribution, as a salesperson you have some say in how this culture of high and low performers operates.

I'll start by assuming you're not at the bottom of your peer group because you're reading this book. If you are struggling, the good news is a focus on Momentum will help pull you out of the muck. Don't worry too much about the rest of this section, you have other work to do. However, if you're somewhere in the middle to top of your group in performance, what I'm about to say about protecting against low performance will be especially interesting to you. Specifically, we are going to talk about establishing and adhering to what I call "minimum acceptable standards" (MAS).

We human beings have a particular talent for finding patterns and telling stories. Therefore it's easy for us to make excuses. If you've been lucky enough to spend time with small children, you can see this in action. Their eyes dart back and forth in their head as they pick out real details from events and make up connections for what happened. "How did the acorn get wedged into the fire pit control mechanism?" asks the parent. "Well," the child said, "I don't know how that happened." They both stare at the seed the repair man just pulled from the firepit. "Wait. I know what must have happened," the child continues. "I was kicking those seeds around the porch … and one may have gone toward the firepit … and must have gone inside there and broke it." The parent and repair man nod their head in unison, marveling at the incredible coincidence.

Knowing this ability to make excuses is practically baked into us, when we as sellers are trying to build some momentum, we need to curb this tendency. We need to set some unimpeachable standards we won't accept. The MAS I referred to previously.

Setting MAS is easy. Keeping them is harder, so resist the temptation to make your MAS too aggressive. For a MAS to work, it must be a true Minimum Acceptable Standard. A result so low, if we were in charge, we would fire ourselves for not achieving. To find the best MASs for building momentum, start with a MAS result and work backward to the originating activity. For instance:

- My personal goal is to sell 10 widgets a month. My quota is 7 widgets a month. My MAS is 3 widgets in a month (the expected result).
- If I fail to hit the MAS of 3 widgets, I should have a minimum of 9 proposals/quotes (activity that should lead to the result happening next).

- If I don't have at least 9 proposals out in a month, I need to have talked to at least 18 prospective clients (activity that should lead to the activity right before the result).
- If I didn't get in front of at least 18 clients I am giving myself 30 days to get back on track (activity that should lead to the activity before the activity before the result).
- If I don't get back on track within 30 days, I need to find another job (the consequence of not meeting your personal MAS).

The example is generic, but the flow isn't. You have personal goals that may or may not be the company's goals for you. These tend to be best case scenarios. Hitting your company's sales goals month after month, quarter after quarter, year after year, is tough to do in most organizations. Your team's best salesperson may not even hit goal year after year.

This has nothing to do with MAS.

Some companies have official MAS in place. Every company has an unwritten MAS in place. Look for the lowest performance over the longest period that didn't result in a firing. That's the unofficial MAS. In companies I work with, the unofficial MAS is often embarrassingly low. And when I ask about its patterns, stories kick in. "How is this person still here?" I ask. "Well, I don't know how that happens," they say. Then we stare at the bad rep's terrible results and lack of activity. "Wait," they say, "I know what must have happened …"

Seriously. It happens. And when you see your leadership team keeping a low performer on staff, it affects your Momentum. So take matters into your hands and create a set of MAS that fits who you're trying to be.

- Stick to the future. Use the company's historical data to help.
- Be generous enough with a low bar that you think, "I would be embarrassed to be that rep."
- Start with results and work back to activity.

Tell yourself it's ok to Fly (see Try, fly, or Die) if you must. You'll be okay. MASs are your friend. If your company doesn't have them, I give you permission to set your own.

One More Thing: I Can't Stand This Software

I mention using company's historical data to set MAS. This requires getting information from the company's customer relationship management (CRM) software. Your company may be forward thinking and have sales operations staff on board who have the job of collecting and analyzing sales-related data. On the other hand, the data may be in the hands of the sales managers or other sales reps. Whatever your situation is, there is one thing I've found in common among companies regardless of size or complexity.

The sales team can't stand the software.

It doesn't matter if they are power users of salesforce or working inside a custom-built application, the complaints are the same. The sales team finds the data entry tedious, and the sales management doesn't trust the data 100 percent.

I am on the side of management when consulting with sales teams. Management pays my bills. Still, take what I'm about to say seriously.

Momentum needs you to take great notes and be amazing at data entry.

The reason it's important is because using the CRM to your advantage makes building Momentum easier. When you lose momentum, excellent data in your CRM will help you pick up speed and get back on track faster.

As I write this book, I am working with a client trying to break through a sales plateau in one of their divisions. This company has the will to grow, the people in place, plenty of funding, and a new service customers value. Despite all that, something is stuck. This is why they've brought me in. I am riding alongside their key people and bringing an outsider's perspective.

From day one, we've been running into a roadblock when trying to answer questions.

The data in the CRM stinks.

As much as we'd like to break through the plateau right now, we are spending all our time going back in time and re-creating data to answer questions. "We should have fixed this sooner," isn't just a lamentation for my benefit, they really feel it. For years they've known this information would be important someday because they have it collected on 20 to 25 percent of accounts. However, no one took responsibility for making sure it was on 75 to 80 percent of accounts instead. This means we are having a hard time working on building the momentum we need to break through the plateau. So far.

The good news is we can get enough information to crack the code and bust through results. The bad news is we must take our time and do a lot of "rework" before we can start in earnest. It's frustrating.

Mr. Carl used to say, "what has happened, will happen." History may not repeat, but it certainly rhymes. At some point you will want the data in your CRM. You will want everyone on your team to have the data in your CRM. You can't demand everyone else is accurate and thorough with data, but you can do your part.

If you're going to keep company culture from hindering your Momentum, it's up to you to model the correct behaviors. This includes updating your CRM software. Even if, as my client's reps tell me, "I can't stand this software."

Be the best one in your group. Keep your data up to date.

Good Stuff in Chapter 9

- Company culture is the set of behaviors the company practices, not the culture defined by the plaque on wall, or front of the employee handbook. These behaviors can aid momentum, or they can hold back momentum.
- From Dillon Allie, the CEO of HDMZ: "Define your culture, hire those that will live it, believe it in it and advocate for it to others, and then get out of the way and let them do their thing."
- You're just one person but you can have an impact on culture. One way is not to allow yourself to impact a co-worker's mood negatively. Once you put this in practice, you can demand your co-workers return the favor. You must earn the right to ask for this.

- Even if your company doesn't use minimum acceptable
  standards (MAS), you can hold yourself to a MAS you define
  on your own.
- Historical data and good notes are your friends when it comes
  to troubleshooting momentum problems. Your momentum
  will get knocked off track for any number of reasons,
  and good data helps the momentum recover faster. Keep
  excellent notes.

CHAPTER 10

Ch-Ch-Ch-Changes— Seeing Challenges Ahead

Overview

It's been said the only constant is change, and this is especially true when it comes to momentum. Staying in motion requires dealing with change effectively, and in this chapter, we talk about awareness, wallowing, proactive autopsying, and using small changes to prepare for larger disruptions.

Change Management: What Has Happened, Will Happen

What has happened, will happen. I mentioned this pithy saying in the previous chapter, and it holds true when we think about how our organization deals with change. The last company element to be aware of as you build (or rebuild) your personal Momentum is in how the company deals with change (see Figure 10.1). If your company is experienced with change and actively works on building resilience, you're less likely to be bumped off track by change. On the other hand, if your company does not consciously work on resilience, it's your job to make plans.

There was an infomercial in the 2000s for an exercise system called P90-X. Every new exercise system needs a unique selling point and this one featured what the extremely fit pitchman called, "muscle confusion." Why would you want to make the same motion over-and-over again, he said. Your muscles start to recognize what you're doing and get more efficient, using less energy. Instead, the P90-X system never settled into one set of exercises. Different muscles and different movements created muscle confusion. The lack of muscle efficiency was the point. Your body would go into high fat-burning mode to keep up. Thanks, P90-X!

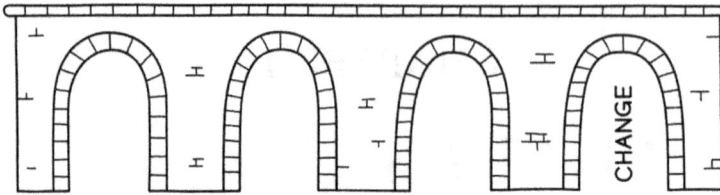

Figure 10.1 Change in the momentum aqueduct

I doubt these claims were scientifically verified, but the concept works for learning how to deal with change. When you are going through change, forced to alter your routine even a little, you become a little more focused. When your routine never changes, days blend into each other and the slightest obstacle knocks us off track.

This is why I say your company should be building resiliency to change. To build Momentum you need routine, but you also need to be in an organization where changes can be dealt with, so if you get knocked off track you recover quickly. To quote a book written with this concept in mind, "*Who Moved My Cheese,*" by Spencer Johnson, "… we resist change because we're afraid of change." We need to know our organization is not afraid of change.

How do you know if your company is ok with change? Let's start by talking about how you'd know what a company that trains on resilience acts like. It's not like they're printing it up in your onboarding documents. It's more subtle than that. Your organization's ability to be resilient is close to its ability to express a clear vision of the future you're working toward. If they know where they are today, and have a picture of where they'll be tomorrow, this is good.

The problem, if there is one, is in how they talk about the in-between part. The part I call the "Black Box of Ambiguity" (see Figure 10.2).

You see, everyone likes the idea of the future, but no one likes the unknown stuff they have to navigate in between where they are today, and where they want to be tomorrow. If your organization expresses a clear path, "if we just do this, we're guaranteed to get that," it may be a sign that they haven't built up their resilience muscle. I teach a course to high school students called, "Introduction to Business and Entrepreneurship." We use a textbook from Steve Blank who teaches an advanced

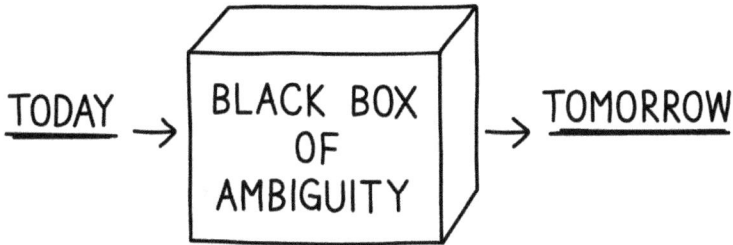

Figure 10.2 The black box of ambiguity

version of the class at Stanford University. He loves to say, "No business plan survives first contact with a customer." I agree. As a salesperson you are the point of interaction between the business plan and the customer. You are where the rubber meets the road, so to speak. In this role, you get firsthand experience with how hard it's going to be to realize the vision of the company. You live in the Black Box of Ambiguity.

You know the plan is subject to change. It is the only thing you can depend on.

If your leadership isn't soliciting feedback, isn't riding along to hear what customers have to say, and hasn't changed a compensation plan or marketing plan in over two quarters, there's a good chance they aren't thinking about resilience.

"Greg, my favorite part about this place is that the comp plan hasn't changed in years," is lovely to hear, but can be bad for Momentum. Remember what we just talked about. The Black Box of Ambiguity is opaque. No one really knows what goes on in there. It's a bunch of squiggly lines, not a straight path (see Figure 10.3).

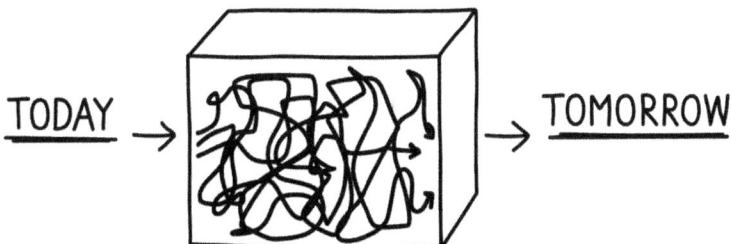

Figure 10.3 Inside the black box

When change happens, it's going to be a mess. Since you're focused on Momentum, keep this in mind. Do something about it.

Let's cover some strategies for dealing with change.

Dealing With Change: Autopsy Now

The first of the two ways you as a salesperson can build your own resilience is to use a technique called "autopsy" now. As you know, an autopsy is an examination done after a death to determine the cause of death. While we don't expect to have a dead body to examine right now, we know how good we are at making up stories. This technique is about making up a story about a future event. Specifically, we're going to make up a story about not reaching the vision. We're going to imagine coming up short, then autopsy now to find out why we didn't make it.

As a rule, salespeople are optimistic. To get out there and talk to people about something that may or may not help them is hard. It's even harder knowing how many bad salespeople there are. There's a good chance the prospect you're talking to has talked to dozens of bad salespeople before you, a great salesperson, comes along.

It makes selling hard.

To deal with this challenge, you tend toward optimism. "It just takes one," is something an optimist thinks.

"Let's pretend this effort failed and imagine a list of the reasons this didn't work," is not something an optimistic salesperson thinks about.

To be resilient to change, however, autopsy now is a great technique for being able to roll over changes and keep your Momentum.

It's a simple technique. Let's get into an example.

We missed our target. Let's talk about why it happened. What is probably reason #1? What could be reason #2? And so on.

It's how this book came about. I want to help you build a burst of impressive Momentum to bridge between your Inspirational motivation to our second form of Motivation, Continuation. If that's the goal and I know what it looks like, I have enough information to get into an autopsy, to do the postmortem, right now with our two-question approach.

We didn't build enough momentum to reach continuation. What is reason #1?

"Something internal knocked me off track."

What are the specific things that happened to knock you off track?

I needed this one big sale to get on track for the quarter and I probably pushed too hard. I wanted the sale more than they needed the product, and I didn't have anything else in the pipeline, so I pressed too hard.

And so on. Work up a short list of obstacles we can think through before they happen. We can address their likeliness to happen and work on preventing them, minimizing their impact, or having a contingent plan for dealing with them when they come up.

It works for strategic planning, and especially for selling in complex environments. It will work for you in dealing with change.

One More Thing: Sharpening the Edge

Another technique you should look for in your company, a technique you can do on your own is sharpening the edge. What I'm about to tell you will sound suspiciously like the exercise program infomercial I mentioned at the beginning of this chapter, because, well, it is the same. Start making changes. Keep yourself just a little on edge, a little bit alert.

When I worked in a call center selling marketing data to sales and marketing teams, each of us managers had about 30 people to keep track of. It was way too many, and each manager developed their own techniques for dealing with it. As I mentioned in the first part of this book, one of my favorite co-workers used to say, "Greg, I like it when my team is a little edgy. When they're kind of uneasy and excited." One of his favorite tactics was to announce some floor-wide event that required everyone to clean up their workstations. This may be a spraying for bugs, or checking all workstations for food, or something similar. The team would clean up their areas before the end of the day and that night he would move everyone around. Whatever reason he gave for cleaning your area was simply a way to make his job easier for introducing change. Most of the excuses didn't make much sense, for instance we worked in a giant, open, modern office and there were no bugs. Although food at your workstation was frowned on, no one was checking. And I'm sure a few of the people working for him would wonder, why are we the only group on the floor doing this?

No matter, the result was as you might expect if you arrived to work tomorrow and your desk was moved. At the time we had a motivational speaker named Larry Winget talk to us. He called himself an "irritational speaker" and he was/is very funny. He has a bit where he imitates an employee saying, "but Larry, you don't understand … they moved my desk!" and I'm sure our teams thought we put him up to it. We didn't, it's just his point and my friend's method were the same. Their intention is the same. Get over it. Things change.

Let's dig into why it worked. First, let me address what's probably in your head. Doing something like that is petty. It's annoying. It's unnecessary. It's a waste of time. And it made people furious. For a day. Or a week. Not much longer though, because everyone had goals to hit and really, a moved desk is a sea of similar-looking workstations is not a big deal. His people, and later my people, got over it.

The reason it worked for us is because it was a small, petty, unnecessary change. It was the Hawthorne effect. It helped build a little "muscle confusion" and kept everyone sharp. This was a big deal because the company we worked for was growing very fast and big changes happened often. New comp plans, new product mixes, new markets, new co-workers, and new bosses. These things happened every few months and were very disruptive. By dealing with little changes we saw our teams do better with bigger changes. Look at Figure 10.4.

When change is happening, we take a hit in enthusiasm and effectiveness. For this state to help us, we need to wallow in it just a little before bringing ourselves up out of the muck. I noticed how my friend's team dealt with our crazy company's changes much better than my teams were coping. He received accolades and opportunities for promotion I did not. When I watched him and asked what he was doing, he explained the call center version of P90X to me and why it worked. Learning to wallow in change is good. It's inevitable. It's going to happen. It's bad to wallow for a long period of time. When you aren't ready for change and it happens, you can end up at the bottom of the graph long enough for it to affect

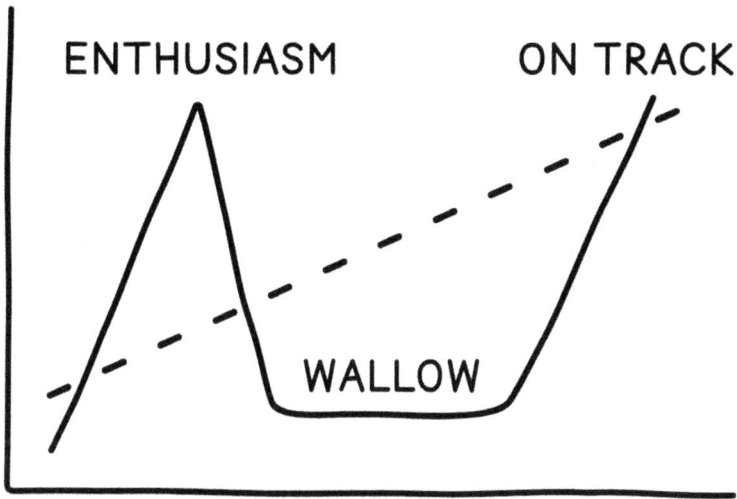

Figure 10.4 Wallowing for just long enough

your job. That's bad. Learning to work through small changes makes dealing with big changes easier.

It keeps you on track for momentum.

If your bosses aren't training you for change, you can force it on yourself. Taking new routes to work. Eating a week's worth of meals with your opposite hand. Changing your wardrobe. There's almost no limit to the number of ways you can introduce change and train yourself to work through it.

The key is to work through it.

You take the same route to work because it's the fastest. You eat with your dominant hand because it's the most efficient. You wear the clothes you wear because they're comfortable. Changing any of these things will create an urge to go back to what you were doing before.

Don't give in! Stick with the change. Live with the discomfort for a while. Figure out a new way.

It works. The next time you face changes in the workplace your training will kick in. While your co-workers wallow in the unfairness of the new territory split, new lead distribution procedure, or—gasp!—new compensation plan, you'll get over it first, and be on your way to identifying a new way to find new customers. Your Momentum won't come to halt as you roll over the obstacle.

You're ready for this. You got this.

Good Stuff in Chapter 10

- Things change. We know this but hate when it happens. Some people and some companies deal with change better than others. They are resilient, as we say. The better you can deal with change, the easier it is to keep momentum going.
- We learned from the Hawthorne Effect that no matter what the change is, we'll eventually learn to live with it. The shorter the time between the change and getting back on track is how we measure resilience.
- One way to shorten your time between change and recovery to stay on track with your goal, is to do a pretend autopsy on why you missed it. By asking what happened before it happens, you can make a short list of obstacles to avoid or prepare for, keeping your momentum going.
- Another way to shorten your time between change and recovery is to practice a version of "muscle confusion" in your daily life. Take a new way to work. Try a new restaurant for lunch. Break the routine. Learning to live with small changes keeps you on track when bigger shocks to the system happen, protecting your momentum as it builds.

PART 4

What a Sales Momentum Mindset Looks Like

Figure P4.1 Putting it all together

CHAPTER 11

The Best Time to Start Is Now—Implementing a Sales Momentum Mindset

Overview

The previous sections have outlined a framework for thinking and talking about Sales Momentum, and in this section, we move into the steps for implementing a Sales Momentum Mindset. The key to implementation is focusing on behaviors more than results. Since salespeople are paid on results, this is harder than it sounds.

Up to now we've been covering the situations that rob us of Momentum. I talk about using these situations to your advantage, but let's face it. Something like a health problem is going to knock you off course more than superior health is going to keep you on track.

That said, we're on the same page now. You have an awareness of what will keep you from building Momentum (see Figure 11.1). What do you do with this information?

In my consulting practice, I see a recurring result that gives me encouragement for any challenge my clients bring me in to help with.

You don't need a lot of Momentum to build before Continuation motivation kicks in.

I experienced this in an early sales job. I've always worked in sales, but it took some time for me to put things together. I was successful in retail sales at a bicycle store, but that only required me to be present to win. Most of the people walking into a bicycle store were ready to buy

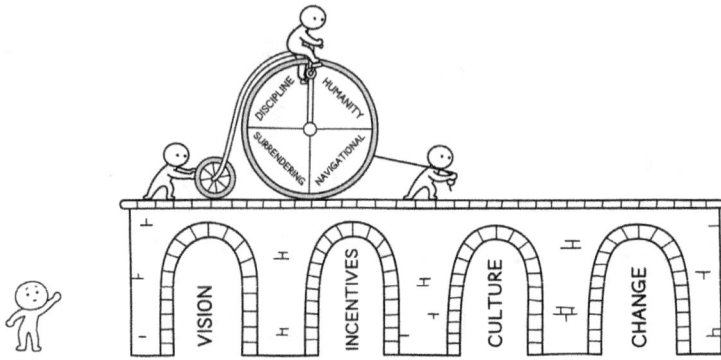

Figure 11.1 Working the momentum flywheel on the aqueduct

something. From there I went to insurance sales. Life insurance to be precise. The training was top notch, but it was a competitive environment, and I had a hard time with the particular kind of rejection that comes from sitting at a kitchen table with prospects. Less successful. From there I did advertising sales. The least glamorous kind of ad sales out there: local print coupon sales. Not successful.

The last three jobs all happened in a two-year period. By the time I went to my marketing database sales job, friends and family asked, is sales really for you? It was a good question. I knew I didn't like to wait for prospects (retail), I didn't do well at the kitchen table (direct sales), and I had trouble in a tiny company (two founders and me—ad sales). By this time, I had read dozens of books, attended hours of training, and developed my own ideas about what worked for me and what didn't. Getting into the right company made a difference because I walked into something with a momentum of its own. There were a dozen successful people on my team. I started by taking aim at the top guy, Vern. I couldn't match his production, but I could get to work a little earlier than him. Stay a little late. I could ask a million questions. I was motivated enough to show up every day. I just needed to start getting small wins. I needed to build Momentum.

Where to Start: New Hires Are Pure

The division I joined at the time had been together for years. It was an old product, but a new product manager was adding a revolutionary piece of technology to it. CDROMs. The old division was going to have some new life and I was in the first group of five new hires.

The thing about new hires, like me at the time, is we don't know what we don't know. We get sold on the vision of the company and whatever they tell us, we believe. We don't have years of missed promises, false starts, and revised policies. There is nothing to ruin our Momentum because we don't have any.

When I met my co-workers in the division, I came in with some ideas about how to deal with them. Remember my story about the catering employee who took me to the races on my first day of work? I wish I could tell you that was the only time I was taken in and led astray by an experienced employee. The lesson I was learning the hard way, is when you're new you need to believe nothing you hear and half of what you see. Instead, you need to focus on the task of building your momentum. You don't need to be motivated. You're new. You need to start stringing together some small wins, get to where you can start to "respect the streak" as we've said before.

What if you're not a new employee? If you're not new and you're looking to regain your Momentum, look to the new employees. See them and think about the things you'd tell them if it were you. Not the negative things, but how to take advantage of the opportunity.

Whatever you come up with is what you need to hear to rebuild your Momentum.

The magic of a new hire, a new recruit, the newbie, is they are ready for Momentum to build.

Chunk It Down: Sprint Sprint Sprinty Sprint

When I started at this job I'm describing, I was told to subscribe to a newsletter called *Tele-Sales Tips* by Art Sobczak. This was before e-mail was widely adopted, so it arrived in the mail. In one of the first issues, Art talked about how to have your best year ever, listing a series of questions you could answer from the point of view of someone who just had their Best Year Ever. What did it look like? What did it sound like? What did it smell like?

I answered all the questions. I set it aside. I had no idea where I put it.

It didn't matter, by doing the exercise I had an idea of where I wanted to finish and it was basically just ahead of the number one salesperson in my division. I took all his stats, all his results, and added 10 percent. I figured what commission might be and imagined what I'd do with all those dollars. I looked at his awards and imagined how they'd look on my desk.

Then I got to work. If he got in at 7:30 a.m., I was there at 7:15. If he left at 5:15 p.m., I left at 5:30. If he made 60 calls, I made 70.

It wasn't very inventive, I just borrowed his life and tried to improve on the metrics I could see.

Here's the point. I caught him. It didn't take long. I mentally planned for a marathon, but it ended up being a sprint. I didn't think I'd come close to beating him for years, but I knew the approach would probably let me match him at some point. It happened in under a year.

This isn't unique to me. This happens with most of my clients too. Once we start focusing on building Momentum, the results show up way faster than expected. It's the sprint nature of Momentum. As Anchorman character Ron Burgundy might say, "Sprint, sprint, sprinty, sprint."

I've learned that it's not useful to think of Momentum as a forever state. It's much better to think of it as a sprint. Or a series of sprints. Stringing together a series of small wins does a lot to build into a big win.

Building Momentum: Forget Maintenance

The key to Momentum is focusing on the build, not the maintenance. The maintenance happens naturally. Remember our second type of Motivation, often confused with the first? This is what I see when I work with salespeople, business development people, principles, and partners. The early motivation, Inspiration, is always there. If you showed up to work, you're inspired enough. What you want is to bridge Inspiration to Continuation. That's what a Momentum focus does for you. It helps you move into productivity and once you get the process down, once you turn building momentum in your own best practice, you won't have to worry about maintaining it.

To illustrate this Momentum phenomenon of stringing together sprints, let's go back to my efforts to be the top salesperson in my little department. If you remember, when I left off, I had started making some gains on the old man of the department. I was consistently getting better results than the women who would come in second or third place each month behind Vern but had trouble staying ahead of him week in and week out.

Then a storm happened. Both literally and internally. Our little city was besieged by an early October snowstorm. It took out power in most of the city and trees, most still holding their leaves, were falling all over the city taking down power lines. The tree in front of my house missed the power lines but took out my car. Squashed it. Instantly totaled.

When I took you through the list of internal momentum controls the list didn't come from some invention in my head, it has been born from experience. That month I experienced most of the issues we've been identifying:

Financially I wasn't ready for a crisis, and we moved in with my in-laws.

Physically I wasn't ready for three days of snow shoveling and threw out my back.

I didn't have a Mentor in place to guide me through these challenges.

I was surrounded by doom and gloom sharing living space with an unhappy wife, mother-in-law, and round-the-clock negative news blasting in my ears.

Emotionally I was a wreck. Volatile and unhappy.

That month and the next month my production fell off dramatically. It was so bad I can still see myself, sitting in the company parking lot, in my father-in-law's car, eating fast food, and crying. With perspective I know today that things weren't so bad, but at the moment it felt like my world was coming apart. Like I didn't deserve nice things.

These challenging months were leading to the Christmas season. My second month of no production was the Christmas commission check, putting more pressure on.

I would love to say I figured things out immediately, but it took months. Extra hours, extra effort. My manager was concerned, as he should be, but to make matters worse he increased our frequency and intensity of meetings. Far from being a sherpa guiding me out of a troubling situation, he was like a roadblock with his constant Inspirational drumbeat. He used to play football in college, and he dug deep into his well of coach speak and Go Get 'em Tiger cheers, often sending me multiple notes a day.

None of that worked. What did work was getting my wheel back in balance and letting momentum build.

Moving in with my in-laws, while initially depressing, cut expenses dramatically, shoring up the checking account.

A neighbor asked me to help him coach a youth basketball team, leading to a lot of running and losing some weight.

I started confiding my situation to this neighbor, and he served as a guide asking questions and offering good, generic advice about my behaviors.

I started spending my lunch hour at the library, reading business magazines and success stories.

My mood improved.

This led to another Momentum build. The company had a vision of getting to a billion in sales (we were just over $100 million at the time), the culture rewarded selling, and I had wallowed in the muck just long enough to see it as temporary. I still had my "best year ever" ideas in mind and I got back in action.

This is why I tell you Momentum isn't a forever/always on experience. It's useful to imagine a rolling stone endlessly going downhill, picking up speed, and crushing obstacles along the way, forever, but it's not going to happen this way. Your momentum, like motivation, is going to ebb and flow over time. The usefulness of these Momentum concepts is when we focus on building or maintaining momentum, our periods where momentum disappears get smaller and smaller. Your ability to pick momentum up and build it again gets easier and easier.

Lots of Hits: Small Changes Add Up

The way momentum builds is stringing small hits together. As professional baseball player Aaron Rowand said, "You have to string together hits." Let me share a screenshot of a tool I use to keep my weight in check.

What is more powerful than seeing progress?[1] I am writing this chapter as I watch Major League Baseball's 2022 World Series. Two of the best

---

[1] R.H. Thaler and C.R. Sunstein. 2009. *Nudge: Improving Decisions About Health, Wealth, and Happiness* (New York, NY: Penguin Books), pp. 92–93.

teams in baseball trying to string hits together or prevent the other team from stringing hits together.

The grid presented in Figure 11.2 is from Weight Watchers. In 2021, as a beach vacation approached, I took a particular interest in keeping my weight in check. If you're unfamiliar with Weight Watchers, it essentially asks you to answer one question each day: "Did you eat your recommended amount of food today?" In October last year, I didn't have a lot of good eating days in a row but compared to months earlier I strung some hits together. And it worked; 30 percent of the month eating well versus 0 percent (or worse, an unknown percent) helped me slim down. We're not talking miracle weight loss, but my belt certainly noticed.

One of the keys to using Momentum in sales is this idea of small streaks. Small changes add up to big results. Trying to string a few good days together each week to make progress for the month. My October measures may not show many streaks, but I was consistent every week. It works.

Figure 11.2 Tracking progress

Going back in time again, as I emerged from my dark period after the October storm, this getting on a roll was my focus. I knew where I wanted to go, I just needed to string together a few good days. When I missed a day, I didn't let it bother me, I simply tried to not have a lot of bad days in a row. I didn't have the Weight Watchers app to illustrate my progress, but I did have a yellow legal pad to keep notes on. I remember looking back day after day and my notes showed me a similar pattern to today's tracking apps. Being on target two or three days a week, and not missing a week of these small hits was what brought me back from the brink. Within a couple of months, I was recognizing new opportunities and setting new sales records. This is in no small part to my focus on building and maintaining momentum.

Baseball player Aaron Rowand's full quote is, "You have to string together hits. You can end up with 16 in a game, but if you get two per inning you might not score a run. It's about stringing them together."

String some hits together. Make the small changes add up by stacking them on one another. You don't need to be perfect every day, but you do need to try. As Mr. Carl would say, "Did you do your best today?" If I said yes, he would tell me that's all we can ask for. If I hesitated, he'd jump in and tell me to try again tomorrow.

Good stuff.

Good Stuff in Chapter 11

- Focusing on momentum yields results faster than you'd expect. The trick is to focus on the process and stick with it. Calling them "momentum sprints" helps keep us on track.
- Momentum emphasizes behavior and activity more than results. By aiming at consistent activity and putting an emphasis on "being there" rather than "being good" you'll make things happen.
- Limiting the time spent wallowing in bad results takes practice. You can prepare your mind for it, but when you're caught in the riptide, so to speak, it's hard to remember not to fight it, but swim parallel to the shoreline. That said, those

safety announcements the airlines make are better preparation than nothing. Make yourself aware.

- Tracking stats and taking notes do wonders for helping you break from a bad spell. Be consistent with your activity tracking and note taking shorthand because reviewing them will reveal secrets to rebuilding momentum.

CHAPTER 12

Managers Are Special— Sales Manager Tools

Overview

Part of being good at sales is being asked to lead a sales team. It's been said the best salespeople make the worst sales managers, but this is only half true. The skillset of a high-performing salesperson is different than the skillset of a high-performing sales manager. This chapter outlines a few thoughts on using a Sales Momentum Mindset to bridge these skills.

In my experience helping salespeople build spurts of Momentum, there is a natural consequence to success.

You will get promoted.

It may be to an advanced sales role like Major Accounts or Special Agent or some sort of title. Or it may be to sales team lead, followed by a chance to be sales manager. In any case, the rewards tend to come in the form of more responsibility. I could write another book about the transition from sales producer to sales manager because this transition happens so many times despite my warnings that the best salespeople do not make great sales managers. Since companies refuse to heed my warnings, I'm left with giving advice on how to change the behaviors that make you successful at selling into new behaviors that make you successful at managing.

If you happen to be in management and picked this book up for ideas on how Momentum can help your sales team, you're in the right place. However, if you jumped straight to this chapter, I warn you that what I'm about to say assumes you've read about the elements of personal momentum and the elements of company momentum. If you are a sales professional who is management curious don't let this chapter dissuade you! Despite my warnings that top salespeople make suboptimal sales managers, there are many of us who figured it out and you will too.

I know this because I needed to make the jump into management. The way our company was set up, it was the next logical step on the rung and I jumped in with gusto. And I was terrible at it. At first. The problem I had was tamping down my enthusiasm to sell, to take action instead of keeping my reps in action. My reps knew I was too eager to sit idly by as they figured out how to work with a prospect. I mean, my mortgage payment depended on these deals getting closed! Plus, it felt to me like my people appreciated my help. In this chapter, I'll cover some of the lessons I learned that turned me from a producer/sales manager into a true middle manager. Lessons I impart to new sales managers as best as I can.

Prima Donnas: High Performers Giveth, and High Performers Taketh Away

Managers love to manage elite, high-performance sales teams. If everyone on the team is meeting or beating quota, the manager is beating quota and getting a nice bonus check every quarter. The problem with this ideal is it doesn't happen that way. Most of the time you have a top producer or three that make up 80 percent of your quota and the bulk of your sales team makes up the other 20 percent. The Pareto Principle in action.

These high performers used to be you. You have an affinity for anyone who can consistently come in and make their numbers. They're a joy to work with. They have Momentum. You don't need to worry about their motivation because you know they are motivated to keep it going.

You just need to Motivate those bottom performers to get up and running.

Here's what I've learned about Momentum and top performers. If a sales manager is hands off with their top performers, the Momentum of the bottom performers never gets built. This doesn't make sense on the surface, but there is something about a top performer having earned the rights of success that is demotivating to everyone unable to reach quota.

I don't have a grand unifying theory for why this is, I've simply experienced it and noticed it. I have been around top performers as a low performer, I have been a top performer, and I have managed top performers. A hands-off approach to managing them results in reinforcing the Pareto Principle. It gets hard to break the 80/20 cycle. A hands-on approach to managing them turns into a battle of wills. Both are a lose–lose proposition.

When I was hired as a regional sales manager my ready-made team came to me with a very high producer, his two close followers, a few fans, and a dozen underperforming sales reps who were on the outside looking in. This top performer was earning four to five times what the average rep in the company brought home and my unwritten instruction from my boss was to keep him happy, no matter what.

Meeting him for the first time it was clear that this was his understanding of how things worked too. In his mind, I was walking into the easiest job of my life. Let him run and reap the rewards. According to him, every manager before had done this and seemed happy.

So why was I there? Because while the highest performing sales rep of all time was on the team, the region was a consistent underperformer. I was the latest in a long line of managers brought in to do something about bringing this untapped territory up to production.

What my all-star producer didn't know was I had just been fired from a management role where I coddled my top producer just as his past managers were coddling him. I came from a situation where she produced sales like no one else had ever done and, despite my instincts, told me to stay out of her business. Did you see the movie "*A Few Good Men?*" starring Tom Cruise and Jack Nicholson? It's a movie about an accident/possible murder on a military base. There's a famous scene where Tom Cruise is the lawyer questioning Jack Nicholson's character, the General. The General can't believe he's been dragged away from his post on the frontier back to the states to face questioning in a court of law, especially by some spoiled schoolboy type who isn't exposed to danger. The General is a top producer. He's out there getting results. Amazing results. When he does his job so well, who has the right to question his methods? Just look at the results. With a snarl on his lips he tells Tom Cruise's character,

"I have neither the time nor the inclination to explain myself to a man who rises and sleeps under the blanket of the very freedom that I provide, and then questions the manner in which I provide it!"

This is what my top producer was like. I needed her production to hit my number and when she delivered time and time again, who was I to question how she did it? I mean, wasn't I getting big commission checks? Wasn't I enjoying the limelight of being on stage and getting quizzed by other managers about how I was making it happen? This led to me ignoring the warnings of her co-workers. It led to me ignoring signs of fraud.

Ultimately, it led to a big mess and we were both let go; she for fraud, me for enabling the behavior.

Fresh off this experience and having had some time to reflect on it, I found myself in a new job taking over this new territory with a similarly successful rep. He was not acting in a dishonest way, but he also wasn't acting like a team player. He had a few friends within the team and under his tutelage they were hitting their numbers. When I walked in, we had to come to an understanding about his success, the team's success, and the company's success. Like Tom Cruise's character I had to weather the bluster and get to the truth. When we got to the truth, we had to learn to trust one another because he needed to protect his Momentum and I needed to build the rest of the team's Momentum. This had to happen without his missing a commission check and without me compromising the company's reputation. We got there by focusing on Momentum. I helped clear the path for him, and in return, he thought about the Momentum of the rest of the team.

High performers can give you a lot and make your job easier, but they can also destroy your collective Momentum. This chapter covers a few ways as a sales manager you can work together to get there. I am not a proponent of making everyone equal. I think you need to play favorites. If you've been lucky enough to inherit a new sales team where everyone is at a similar production level, I'd encourage you not to fight the high–low performer dynamic. It's going to happen naturally. What I encourage all my sales managers to focus on is behaviors and Momentum.

The Sum of the Parts: Group Momentum as a Concept

As an individual producer you are focused on individual Momentum. As a sales manager you are concerned about individuals to a degree, but you are much more interested in Group Momentum.

Group Momentum is the sum of the behaviors of your collective team. You want to make sure your best performer doesn't lose momentum when they look at the lowest performing member, and you want to make sure your bottom performer doesn't look at the preferential treatment of the top and lose pace.

When I started working with my new region, it was easy to see who was at the top and who was at the bottom of production. It was not so easy to see why. The activity levels weren't so different, the product mix wasn't so different, and the understanding of the commission (my go to for an immediate sales boost) wasn't so different. It was hard to see exactly why one guy was able to sell five or six times more, but I knew if we could unlock it for the rest of the region, it would have a ripple effect throughout the entire company.

What eventually came to light was not an internal Momentum element, it was very much external. Well, it was external to him but internal to the company. My superstar rep was incredibly well connected to the company's internal resources, so much so that his new accounts were approved at a much faster rate than anyone else's. The secret to his success was he had taken the time to investigate the entire sales process and worked hard to make everyone's job easier. With his deep knowledge of the various department managers and customer service agents, he made doing business with him easier than dealing with any other company, let alone any other rep in our own company.

Once this came to light, my challenge was extracting his behaviors out and teaching them to the rest of the team. Much like the expert cook in your kitchen, the one that might work from a recipe but knows exactly when to add a little of this or take out a little of that, we needed to pull some of this information out. This is never easy, and especially not easy if your top rep is concerned they may lose their place at the top if they give too many recipes away.

The lessons I learned here are that there has to be a buy in at the top that a rising tide lifts all boats. He needed to know that he would get more financial rewards, but also that he could learn to enjoy the success of others, even if they weren't his closest friends. We all perform better when surrounded by excellence. To use a sports analogy, we play to the level of our competition. It's rare to be the person who is able to stand out when surrounded by incompetence. The law of averages is bound to kick in. Since we know this happens, surround yourself with top performers, or at least higher performers. When the group is building Momentum, it's easier for individual producers to maintain Momentum.

Resistance to Momentum: Culture Eats It, But Keep Serving It Up

Management guru Peter Drucker famously said, "culture eats strategy for breakfast." While this makes culture sound scary, your team member's Momentum relies on the truthfulness of this quote.

Culture is how people act every day. A sales manager who behaves with Momentum as a priority sends a signal to even the most momentum-challenged team member, string together some wins, no matter how insignificant they seem to you right now, because these wins will add up to something significant over time.

This is important because if a manager is bought into this concept, they stop asking for things from the team without pausing to consider how it will affect momentum. Our organization's culture shows our people what's important to them with every action we take. Imagine an analyst who is required to stay up all night to complete a report only to see it in the trash the next morning. What does that have to do with momentum? Well, why ask for it if we don't need it? When we ask for it, then something changes, why not explain what changed?

These little obstacles in momentum are what should keep you up at night as a manager. If you can anticipate them in any meaningful way, your team will make more progress over time than a competitor who doesn't respect momentum.

What can you do when you see behaviors/practices that are cultural norms, but you know can ruin momentum? Like, say, TPS reports that end up in the trash? What do you do then? Your boss wants the TPS report, your team knows no one looks at the TPS report, but if the TPS report isn't done there will be hell to pay?

Don't add to the misery of the TPS report. Use your company's culture to your advantage. Sometimes this means working the behaviors to your advantage, other times it means not letting the behavior become a distraction. I am not telling you to change or challenge the need for the TPS report. I am saying cultural issues that are mole hills can turn into mountains if we're not careful.

Culture eats strategy. Your plans, no matter how impressive or well meaning, will fail if they don't fit what your people do every day. I wrote a whole book about it. Meet your people where they are. Don't make things more complicated. Zig Ziglar used to say, "Don't wish it were different, wish you were better." It fits here. You can't fight City Hall. You can work around it while paying homage to it. Align yourself and your team with your culture. Admit where things could be better, but don't apologize. Build momentum and sustain momentum that is well begun. You'll get further on your Momentum bursts and your team will enjoy more success.

Getting back to my top producer, he built a culture in our territory. It was unwritten and my job was to uncover it and work within it. I couldn't change the culture without him, and the only way to get movement was to meet him where he was and walk with him to a new place.

After you get promoted, as you take over your own sales team, one that is probably populated with your peers from your time in sales, focusing on momentum will set you up for success. Your team is showing up for work each day, so they don't need more motivation. Focusing on momentum to bridge them to Continuation, motivation should be your goal. My top producer sharing his insights with the rest of the region about his skill at managing the company's departments was revelatory. It was brave of him to show us the way, and once he figured out no one, even with his insights, was going to "cook" as well as he did, our region thrived. We still had a bell-curve-shaped performance with him at the far right of the curve, but the hump in the middle came a little further his direction, and did it consistently (see Figure 12.1).

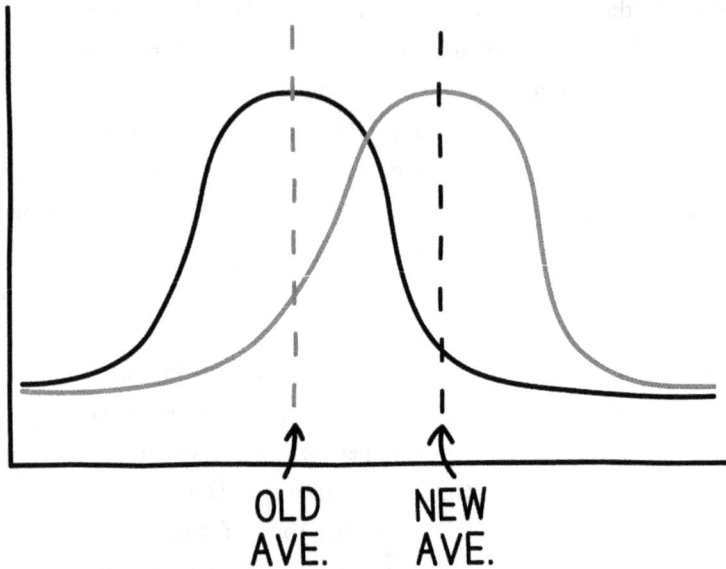

Figure 12.1 Making progress

A culture of momentum does wonders for a team. If you find yourself in a sales management position in competition with other sales managers, I'll put my money on the manager focused on momentum.

Good Stuff in Chapter 12

- Sales managers are special. I don't just say this because I am one. If you do well in sales, your leadership will eventually ask you to be one. A word of warning: selling and managing require different strengths. Prepare yourself.
- Managing high performers is the first place you'll see the need for different skills than you used in being a great seller. Top sellers want to be left alone to do their job. Managers need to know the details of their work. Navigating this conflict is a challenge, but can be done.
- When you think about what needs to be done to bring your group along, it's easy to default to Inspiration. It feels like the answer to everything. Force yourself to look at each of your

people's momentum. Who has it? Who doesn't? What can be done to help them?

- Your team's sales culture can be summed up in one word: Yes. As in, every time you say yes to an exception it becomes the rule. Every time you take an action it becomes a rule.
Be patient.
- Holding your team to a high standard coupled with working to clear the path ahead so they can build momentum is a shortcut to success. Your checkbook will thank you later.

CHAPTER 13

Release the Parking Brake or Rev the Engine— Implementation Strategies

Overview

Implementing a Sales Momentum Mindset involves two skills, reducing restraints or increasing effort, or as I call it, releasing the parking brake or revving the engine. In this chapter, we cover a few more tactics to keep sales momentum front of mind. Once the sales momentum mindset takes over, long-term results get easier to visualize and bring to reality. We do this by taking a high-level look at a company where it's being implemented.

The experts tell us thinking about solutions in a binary, "either/or" orientation is limiting, but it has some advantages, especially when it comes to implementing an idea. The big idea in this book is we need to change our tendency to look for Inspiration and replace it with action, or a tendency toward Momentum. The easiest way to make it happen is to focus on one of two approaches, think in black or white. Our binary orientation is we're going to "rev the engine" or "release the parking brake."

In this chapter, we're going to talk about specific tactics to make Momentum part of your daily routine.

Starting: The Clues Are Everywhere

We are surrounded by triggers. I have some friends with addiction issues and one of the ways they break their behaviors is to sever the trigger. They release the parking brake. Sometimes this means changing a routine, other times it takes more drastic actions like moving to a new city. All to escape certain triggers and find new ones. Anything can be a trigger. I learned this reading B. J. Fogg's book "*Tiny Habits.*" He offered an example of the flushing toilet. With the flushing toilet as a trigger, you have something that happens multiple times a day, which you can use to remind yourself of a new behavior you wish to exhibit. The new behavior he uses in his book is exercise. Flush the toilet—think more exercise. For example, go to the bathroom, flush the toilet, and as you wash your hands you remember, "hey, exercise," so you drop to the floor and knock out five pushups and five sit-ups.

I'm no longer doing the five and five, but like Pavlov's dog, every time I flush I still think "exercise."

To change our thinking to be more oriented to Momentum, let's start by looking for triggers. As our flushing toilet friend tells us, the clues are everywhere.

Make It Easy: Cutting or Stretching Restraints

So, Greg, you ask, how exactly do you cut or stretch restraints (see Figure 13.1)? Good question. For an example, let's look at one segment of our Momentum wheel for how it works. For instance, let's say you're looking at your wheel and you think, "The first thing I'm going to do is make sure my wheel is in balance. I'm going to rate myself on each of these four areas, giving myself a score of 1–10 in the two segments." After completing this exercise, you see one area where you can improve: Intellectual Firepower. You rate yourself an 8 in every area but that

Figure 13.1 Cutting restraints or adding incentives

one, where you've given yourself a 6. Since you know you need a little improvement, what will improvement look like? How will you know you're making progress?

If you tell yourself, "Self, the easiest way for me to improve my intellectual firepower is to read a little bit of a sales-related book every day," that is a strain on restraints, a revving of the engine. You are adding to your already busy day.

You could also say, "Self, social media is making me feel dumber. The easiest way for me to improve my intellectual firepower is to stop looking at it first thing in the morning," that is cutting a restraint, a release of the parking break. You are taking something out of your already busy day.

Both approaches work, and they tend to work together. Cutting out 20 minutes of mindlessly scrolling social media every day, and replacing it with 20 minutes of reading sales books is a great strategy.

If I am advising you, though, my bias is for focusing on the restraint and the corresponding trigger. When you start your day mindlessly scrolling through social media, when does that happen? Are you grabbing your phone before you go use the toilet, scrolling as you do your business? If that's the trigger, what can we do to remind ourselves of our intention? What about putting a sales book in the bathroom? First thing in the morning as you feel nature's call, you see the book and—trigger —you're reminding yourself about your commitment to intellectual firepower.

One reason New Year's resolutions fail to take hold is we are hardwired for shortcuts. Our brains take in a lot of information and sets up shortcuts to deal with this flood of information. This means we ignore most of what our senses pick up. However, if it's novel, we can't help but notice it. Our brains need a novel instance trigger. It's the reason I used the toilet example previously. We want to ignore the mental image of sitting on the toilet mindlessly scrolling through social media, but our brain is like, "hold up! This might be interesting." Spend as much time thinking about what is preventing you from a goal as you spend coming up with the goal. When we add actions to our already overworked brains, we're putting stress on restraints. We're adding to our day. It's more effective to stop doing something.

It reminds me of an old vaudeville joke.

The patient says, "Doctor, it hurts when I do this!" And proceeds to spin his hand around by his elbow like it's on a broken hinge. The doctor looks at the patient for a beat, then says, "Well, don't do that!"

When you work on improving any of the areas of the Momentum Wheel, my advice is to start with cutting behaviors. Create a gap. Open up some space. "Don't do that."

Salespeople are naturally optimistic and get excited about new things. Use that as a trigger. "I am excited to start doing X, what will I stop doing?" Once triggered, get to work figuring out how to stop that thing.

In Your Head: It's Sounds Personal Because It Is Personal

If you've read this far and think,

Greg, I get your point, but I feel like changing my thinking from Motivation to Momentum is a personal thing. I can't imagine telling anyone about things like my finance or health, let alone getting into that Higher Power stuff.

That's right.

The elements of Momentum are personal, but as soon as you start sharing, it gets easier. We've learned to go along with inspiration, the rah–rah exhortations from sales trainers, and listening to personal power gurus because it's easy. But it took time, didn't it? I've had hundreds, maybe a thousand, conversations with sales reps where I end up jumping on the desk and stomping around to get them excited. Once they jump up with me it's only a matter of time before everyone gets comfortable demonstrating enthusiasm. We learn how to do motivation.

But like Jim Rohn says, "Motivation alone is not enough. If you have an idiot and you motivate him, now you have a motivated idiot."

I have often been, and encouraged others, to be motivated idiots.

It's easier than getting personal, because we're familiar with it.

The Momentum Wheel and bridge framework is a way to get used to the personal bits of momentum. It gives us a language and frames the conversation. We're already inspired enough. We need to focus on stringing some hits together. We get there by starting somewhere.

A Case Study

I have a client who is generally unimpressed with my ideas. It sounds harsh, but it's true. He's like a brother to me. We've worked together for years and where I'm off the charts, excited about new ideas, he's just as excited about execution. He's the doubting Thomas to my divine inspirations.

When I approached him with this idea, the idea we spend too much time on inspiration, not enough on momentum, he said, let's try it in my company.[1] So, we did.

His sales force was equally split between veteran producers and new employees. The turnover rate with new employees tends to be high because the established salespeople aren't excited about the new people. "Why invest any time with them if they're just going to leave?" said one of the top producers in a fit of honesty. She's right. Why bother? It may help in some broad sense, but not in her pocketbook.

Fitting Your Momentum Lens

When we tried to focus on the obstacles to the veteran's momentum, we were initially stumped. The top producers have been high-level producers for years. Historically, the biggest challenge is getting them to care about increasing revenue even 10 percent. They already make plenty of money. This is why my friend keeps trying to bring new people on board. He thinks if he's going to grow it won't be through the existing staff. He's given up on the veterans.

---

[1] W. Mattern. 2023. "Review of Momentum in M & D Information Systems Sales Training," *Interview by Gregory Chambers.*

When we look at his new people, their challenges look completely different. The products my friend sells are a mix of product and service. Customers are buying the advice of the salesperson as much as they are buying a specific product. New people, as it happens, don't know enough to be helpful. The momentum obstacles for the new people were easier for us to identify. They could turn to the veterans for help but, as we know, the veterans have no incentive to be helpful. My client wants to hire better self-starters. Find people who are motivated to learn on their own.

Before we could do any work on momentum, we had to deal with this idea of finding the exact right people. Rethinking the ones he hired in the past were just lazy or something. Reconsidering the idea they just need to put in some more work. To try harder. Although he didn't say it out loud, he thought, "veteran producers aren't special, they figured it out. The new people have a motivation problem."

To get over this hurdle, we had to consider all the remedies he's tried for finding better people. Referral bonuses. Increased salaries. Taking salespeople from competitors. Incentives for the first sales. Spending more time on training. More meetings. We concluded that he's tried a lot of motivation-related things. It may not be motivation.

With new hire's motivation set to the side, we could go back into the veteran's business flow to see what they did, specifically, to be so consistent. How they "respect the streak?" We found one reason the veterans produce so consistently is because they have repeat business. Not only do they have customers calling in over and over again, among the veteran producers we discovered an unwritten rule, a hidden rule, that the last person to talk to someone calling in got the new call. In practice this meant that if a customer went dormant for years, then responded to a marketing piece, the person who talked to them five years ago (but never kept in touch) got the opportunity. It worked well for the veterans but was a nightmare for the new people. My client's business has been around for 25 years, and quite a few new calls are from past customers.

Another thing we found veterans have going for them is a steady income. With almost 50 percent of their pay coming from commissions, they know they can depend on that commission coming in. New people are hired with the idea they too can have big commissions, but realistically, those commissions won't be coming in for some time, killing momentum.

The problem was clearer now. With our polarized momentum lenses we could see inside the stream. New people need to get momentum without affecting the momentum of the veteran salespeople. The possible solutions, when viewed through the lens of momentum, were becoming clearer too.

Momentum Case Study Insights

For the veterans, we decided to put them in a "continuation motivation" bucket. It is clear they are respecting their streaks and we needed to keep that going. The way to bring new salespeople along, which could be seen as a threat to veteran momentum, is to invest in more lead generation. There is a natural close rate the veterans have developed over time, and if we disrupt it to the positive, giving them more opportunities, it will be easier for them to continue respecting the streak. The new hires are seen as less of a threat to commissions. Once the new lead generation spend is decided on, we communicated to the veterans, describing it as an investment in them and the business.

For the new people, we changed how he recruits and hires them. In the interviews, we are looking for evidence of a curious mind, because they need to learn a lot to bring value to customers and make sales. If they aren't interested in homework, they might not be a fit. The interviews now come with homework. He is also looking for someone who can live on less to start. We know if they come in and the position puts pressure on their finances right away, they're going to give up. We don't use the veteran's earnings as a job-selling point.

We have also included the veterans in the hiring process. They participate in interviews. Specifically, we have them rate the new hire on culture fit. The veterans also take part in early training and are compensated for it, hopefully exposing the newbies to hidden rules.

As the plan is set in motion, my client and I feel like the momentum lens has given us a unique insight into the business and makes a difference (the plan was put in motion in late 2019).

Actual Momentum Results

Everyone has a plan until they're punched in the face, said heavyweight boxing champion Mike Tyson. For us, the pandemic threw the plan into disarray. The investment in lead generation started in late 2019 and was easy to continue through 2020, but the hiring of new salespeople was put on hold as he transitioned the company to a remote-only workplace. This required a new investment be made in technology to support the remote workforce, and by the end of 2020, we could get on track with hiring. The new remote workplace created turnover as some employees did like it, but there was no impact on sales. The investment in lead generation was paying off, just not as planned. When it came time to hire the next round of new salespeople, the playing field was significantly different. We were forced to find people who could work remotely, in addition to being intellectually curious, and a culture fit.

As I write this in late 2022, we have some results. The company's primary goal is revenue growth and sales are up 25 percent for the second year in a row. With the unexpected move to remote work, general business expenses are lower, and my friend is happy. There is still turnover in the new sales team, but there is now one additional high-producing salesperson, working well with the veterans. It's not dramatic, but it's a start. The new hires are universally more accepted; they have been financially stable; and they are interacting with the veterans much more than ever before because of involving veterans in hiring and training.

The intellectual curiosity is still a stumbling point. The homework concept hasn't been foolproof. We have plans for getting better by making the hiring process include a greater emphasis on using the probationary period as a true probation. It's better to part amicably on the front end of the relationship before momentum starts, than for a new hire to leave after fits and spurts of momentum give everyone hope.

The next challenge is keeping the "new" middle of the road veterans in motion while we find more salespeople. Besides the one new high producer, there are four more middle-of-the-road producers we need to work with. To start with, we are training on the concepts of this book. As we've said, momentum is personal so we're working on helping everyone focus on momentum via their own efforts, not relying on the company.

They're learning to be more about the thumb than the finger!

Another saying, from one of my many managers (not Mr. Carl this time) is, "it's a process, not an event." The momentum lens is all about process. Inspiration is all about the event. This is going to be a process … not an event. Profound stuff.

Good Stuff in Chapter 13

- Putting momentum thinking into practice is easier when you look for one of two opportunities. Either cut a restraint, or add energy to anything that's working.
- When you see a place where you can "rev the engine" or "release the parking brake," before acting, look for a trigger. Attaching your action to a trigger helps with implementation.
- Our minds are attracted to novelty. The best triggers are based on novelty. So the more improbable, funny, colorful, smelly, scary, or stupid, the better.
- Using a momentum lens, troubleshooting sales problems gets easier. It forces you to look away from the result and dig into the process leading up to the results. Even going back to your hiring process.
- "It's a process, not an event." My momentum lens is saying this is its most favorite saying ever.

CHAPTER 14

Restarting Momentum

Overview

The nature of continuation motivation is it's hard to pin down when you're experiencing it, but easy to recognize when it's gone. In this chapter, we talk about the inevitable loss of sales momentum, and how our sales momentum mindset helps us troubleshoot efforts to get it back. The nature of momentum is action, and it's through action that we resurrect sales momentum and get back to the revered state of continuation motivation.

Part of using our momentum lens is recognizing when momentum is gone. It happens. The streak is interrupted for some reason. Maybe it's an unexpected run of expenses. It could be a health problem. It could be the health and finances of a loved one. I've seen bad advice from a mentor slow momentum down. Same with the loss of a support system or a support system turned toxic, like in a divorce. Other times, it happens to our company like a new competitor putting pressure on a core product. Or learning that your company's incentive program is not at generous as a competitor's. Company cultures can turn negative, or a newly promoted manager can be a challenge. Whatever happens, momentum gets affected. It feels like we're no longer in motion.

What do we do?

Let's talk about what happens when our momentum lens shows us at a stop, but we're just not that excited about doing the work.

Self-Sabotage: The Beastie Boys Knew It All Along

I'm at a football tailgate with my brother-in-law and a group of our friends-in-common. I haven't seen this group for a decade, but within minutes we're falling back into our old banter. Before smartphones and having access to the world's knowledge at our fingertips, we used to have ridiculous debates that went on for hours. The topics varied, but someone would take a position on a topic and we'd spend the night trying to come up with a way to either support or refute their stance. On this day, we revert back to our old habits and tailgate talk turns to music videos. (Tailgating, for the few of you who may be unfamiliar, is hanging out in the parking lot before a game. It's key feature is passing time through random conversation, playing parking lot games, or both.) The debate about best music video ever is discussed and, on this day, one of us claims, "the Beastie Boys 'Sabotage' video is the best ever." I bring this up because my number one reason for momentum coming to a halt is self-sabotage. We're either neglecting part of our flywheel, or we've done something to knock ourselves out of balance. Even if there's a perfectly pitched aqueduct stretching out in front of us, we can't roll. We've done something to our flywheel that stops action and brings our momentum to a halt.

Part of the goal of this book is to give us a language for troubleshooting this exact situation. Either by ourselves or with a trusted third party, we walk through the four parts of our personal flywheels or look at the companies we work for and can diagnose a problem. When we have lost momentum, the first step is admitting there is a problem and identifying it. With this book as a guide, we can get to work.

The way I was taught to troubleshoot business problems is after identifying the problem, get back to the exact spot where divergence from the expected norm happened[1] (see Figure 14.1).

This divergence isn't the easiest thing to find, especially when it's us trying to pinpoint some form of self-sabotage, but it's an excellent way to get yourself back on track. I'm partial to using third-party professionals for this work. A good therapist is armed with a battery of excellent questions and superior listening skills to help us identify where we got off track. Especially if they are willing to work within the framework you outline. In years of recommending therapy, I've learned that not everyone

---

[1] C.H. Kepner and B.B. Tregoe. 1965. *The Rational Manager: A Systematic Approach to Problem Solving and Decision Making* (New York, NY: McGraw-Hill), pp. 73–87.

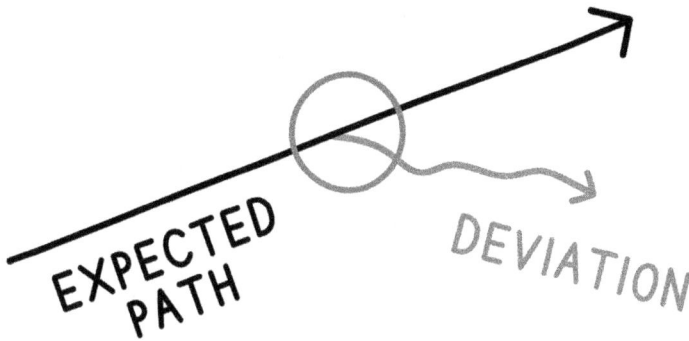

Figure 14.1 Problem solving by finding the point of deviation

is a fan of the practice. It's a lot like talking about mimes! There are strong feelings around therapists. So, if you are against therapy, I have another recommendation. Writing. Especially the practice of freewriting.

If this sounds more like you, I suggest you pick up a book, "*Accidental Genius: Using writing to generate your best ideas, insight, and content*," by Mark Levy. He outlines a way to do a version of what a good therapist does, in the comfort of your own home. The easiest way I can explain freewriting is you set an uninterrupted time like 20 minutes, you put yourself in front of a blank sheet of paper or empty document on your computer, you give yourself a topic, and you write. Write as fast as you can without stopping and thinking about punctuation, spelling, grammar, quality of ideas, audience, or anything except the topic. When the timer goes off, set the gobbledygook you just wrote aside for a day or so. After a day, revisit what you wrote. Somewhere in there is the thing that will help you.

I've used freewriting to identify where things got off track, ideas around how to get back on track, and to dream up ways around obstacles both real and perceived. I've used the technique to help clients, to deal with difficult sales situations, and even for writing this book. Done correctly, it's a great way to get past your conscious mind and get into the details of your problems. It's a great way to restart momentum when you've been self-sabotaging your effectiveness.

And it's even more powerful when used in combination with long walks.

The magic of long walks has been noted by poets and philosophers alike. We are kinetic creatures and we benefit from being in motion.

I have a neighbor that comes by my house on regular walks. Like a lot of the walkers trapsing through the neighborhood, he comes by wearing his white earbuds and often looks lost in thought. At a party I asked him what he likes to listen to. Podcasts? Music? He smiles and says,

> Greg, I don't listen to anything. I like to walk and think about things, but people are so friendly they want to stop and talk. With earphones they don't bother. I might get a wave here and there, but I've learned no one bothers me when they see those little white earbuds.

I took his advice and started doing the same thing. It feels a little antisocial, but combined with the freewriting exercise, walking with your thoughts has a way of clearing the cobwebs and bringing novel thoughts to the front of mind. When it comes to problem solving, the freewrite and the walk do an amazing job of helping you identify where you might be stuck, why you might be stuck, and how you might get unstuck.

Whether you use a professional third party or tap into your brain via freewriting, identifying the problem, and where you went off track is the best way to get back on track.

Looking Ahead: Jump-Starting Momentum

When you've been on a roll and reaped the rewards of momentum, then lost it, the rebuilding process can look daunting. Even if you know exactly where and when the problem started.

Don't worry. You're eyes aren't deceiving you, it is daunting!

I'm going to give you some advice here that may seem counterintuitive. If you have done the troubleshooting, identified the problem, and found the point of divergence. Then you've come up with some ideas on how to get back on track and when you start to do the work, just don't feel the inspiration, don't panic. Get in motion. Act like you have momentum.

It's not as common anymore, but you're probably familiar with cars that have manual transmissions. My first car, my wife's first car, and our kids' first cars have all been manual transmissions. A feature of these cars is they can be started when the battery dies. My first car was an old pickup truck and the electrical system had issues, so the roll push start was a regular part of my life. To make it work, the ignition needs to be in the on position, the transmission needs to be neutral, the clutch needs to be disengaged, and you need to be able to get the car rolling. The details aren't as much fun as the experience I'm about to describe. With the car in motion, I would put the car in second gear, and release the clutch. This sequence of events forces the engine to turn over and roar into life as the truck lurches forward. When the engine starts, you give it a little gas and bam! Your engine is running.

The reason I bring this up is because sometimes the inspiration part of motivation just isn't there. The battery is dead. As Shane Parrish who writes an investment newsletter called "Farnam Street" said,

> If you wait until you're motivated, you've already lost.
>
> Surgeons don't always feel like doing surgery. Teachers don't always feel like teaching. Parents don't always feel like cooking. Firemen don't always feel like rushing into a burning building.
>
> If you let motivation dictate your actions, inertia conspires to keep you in place.
>
> Action creates progress. Progress creates momentum. Momentum creates motivation.[2]

Just like the car sputtering to life, sometimes to get going again you need to push start yourself. You need to focus on action. Taking one step, then two, then three, then four. When you've lost momentum but know what it felt like to have it, you are like the surgeon, teacher, or fireman in his example. You know what you should be doing, but for some reason you've come to a halt. The trick is to force the action.

Let' revisit this app concept again. The power of the tracking system I experienced with the Weight Watchers app comes from it reminding me I don't need to be perfectly in motion every day as much as I need to stay in motion over time. Four days a week is pretty good. Three is okay too.

---

[2] S. Parrish. 2023. *Momentum Creates Motivation*. Farnam Street. https://fs.blog/brain-food/january-8-2023/ (accessed March 4, 2023).

But three or four days a week for three out of four weeks is where the magic really happens. Staying in motion and tracking your activity will get you back in motion. Once you've been inspired the first time and translated that into results, you can forget about relying on inspiration again.

Technology is a great help for keeping us in motion, at times like this. But it's only effective if it's replacing versus adding. The theme of cutting an activity instead of adding a new activity has been mentioned in previous chapters. New technology fits into this idea. If a new technology catches your eye and promises to help you do more, ask yourself one question. "Is this a stand in for an activity I'm already doing?" If the answer is yes, use it. If the answer is "no," or "no but," don't use it.

In Greg's iconography, new technology is represented by a robot. The idea of it standing in for a piece of your process is represented in Figure 14.2.

The robots are best used to cut restraints. Let me give you an example. I get approached by salespeople pushing new sales appointment setting technologies on a weekly basis. A recent one is adamant about showing me their Artificial Intelligence-powered LinkedIn prospecting tool. It does look interesting, so I take the appointment. The salesperson shares a screen with me so I can see how the software works in real time. To demonstrate its power, she starts by asking for my target market. I tell her, she plugs in my criteria, and it comes up with an impressive-looking list inside LinkedIn that matches or comes close to my target. The software combs through my website, the LinkedIn profile of the target market, my LinkedIn profile, and comes up with suggested approach text that looks like something I might say. The rep tells me that once I tweak/

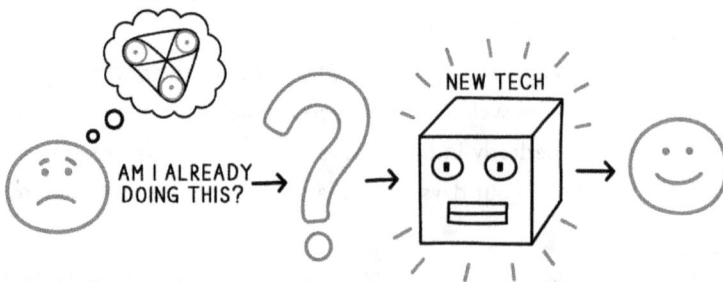

AM I ALREADY DOING THIS?

NEW TECH

Figure 14.2 Using technology for momentum

approve the text it will launch a five-step approach sequence that includes e-mailing their corporate address, using LinkedIn's mail system, and prompts for me to leave a voicemail, along with suggested language for the voice message. She tells me I'm guaranteed four new appointments a week. It's very impressive.

And nothing like my selling sequence.

It reminds me of the example of the futuristic snow blower I mentioned. This is the prospecting tool version of that. And like my example, I might as well be living in the sunbelt and she is selling a snowblower. Would I like another four qualified appointments a week? Sure. But I'm a solo boutique consultancy. I bring on as much work as I need when I need it. I don't use LinkedIn for prospecting. My website isn't exactly updated with the work I do on a day-to-day basis. This tool wouldn't cut any restraints in my business. It's the equivalent of adding triple inspiration!

Now, compare that to the little robot tool inside my newsletter software. After writing my weekly newsletter, I put it up on my website. This process includes a lot of copy/pasting and takes me a few minutes each week. Despite the minor time commitment, I can't seem to get it done on time. As a result, these blog posts pile up on one another and what takes a few minutes now takes a few hours to complete. Mind numbing work. Someone sent me a tool that does the mind-numbing part for me. It takes my newsletter and creates a draft blog post, sitting in my website content management system waiting for my approval to post. What never got done, now gets updated once a month because the robot does 90 percent of what I've been doing giving me time to finish this book!

When you're trying to get momentum back and can't find inspiration, take action. Motion has a way of helping you reclaim momentum. If you struggle to act, look for technology to do some of the work for you, cutting a restraint. And if that doesn't work, consider something more dramatic.

Time Away: The Pause That Refreshes

Occasionally, you may find none of the tricks are getting you back to starting a streak. If you're at a loss for what to do next, consider doing nothing.

Sales can be exhausting. Managing a sales team can be exhausting. Hitting quota month in and month out isn't easy. In the press for more and more, there are times when you need to do less. Cut all the restraints, so to speak. Take the pressure off yourself and check out.

It's a radical idea, I know. The interesting part is, it works.

The test of its effectiveness came during the pandemic. So many of us were forced out of momentum it forced a recognition of sorts. Is this what we're meant to do? What exactly are we trying to do anyway?

This forced reckoning did something interesting to us.

Once we let go, I mean really let go, it kicked a bare bones activity into gear.

Take this book, for instance. It has been in the back of my head for years. Buried. I didn't know just how deep until the darkest days of 2020. A series of speaking engagements were canceled, some clients delayed work, and I had time on my hands. Time I didn't want to fill with work. I let go. Fielded a couple of full-time job offers, and spent a lot of time digging in the dirt. Literally. I was out in the garden trying to enjoy the fresh air and making messes. It reminded me of the task of rebuilding sales momentum that I've talked to clients about over the years. That reminded me to jot down some of the ideas I had, and a book my wife had lying around the house offered an outline I could plug my ideas into. I sent a proposal off to the publisher and got to work.

The only way this happens is if I unplug and clear out the task list staring me in the face. I'm all for building momentum. I'm a huge fan of rebuilding momentum. I also know that sometimes the way to get there is to stop trying so hard.

It's scary, but it works. I swear.

Good Stuff in Chapter 14

- Losing momentum is no fun. Before doubling down on rebuilding momentum, take time to figure out what went wrong and when. It will make maintaining momentum easier in the near future.
- Seek professional help for troubleshooting a loss of momentum. It works. If you aren't sure about therapy or

haven't found the right therapist, consider freewriting and long walks. It also works.

- Action triggers your continuation motivation. When all else fails, if you know what you should be doing, concentrate on doing it over and over. Momentum will develop and a new motivation may just be around the corner.
- If nothing is working to regain momentum, you may be left with doing nothing. Clearing the deck for a while may kickstart some long dormant action. It's not guaranteed to happen, but it's been known to happen. Try everything else first.

CHAPTER 15

Closing Thoughts

Overview

Final thoughts about a Sales Momentum Mindset (see Figure 15.1). The value of any idea is implementing it and reaping its promised rewards. In this concluding chapter, we cover ideas about the value of shifting your mindset and your immediate next steps to make it happen in the real world.

The Fragility of Momentum

As a 13-year-old, I was lucky to be part of a Little League baseball team that experienced some success on the field. The way the Little League end-of-season tournaments were organized, you played an entire season (a lot of games), if you win your team goes to what they called "Districts," playing another series of games to determine who represents your district at State. Our team not only made it to the State tournament, but we also won. After State we were sent to the regional tournament where we played against the other state tournament winners for a chance to go to the Little League World series.

The first team we played at the regional tournament were giants. Comparing their 13-year-old physiques to ours suggested they may be pushing 20. Some of them even had facial hair! Between the long season and the Goliaths from our neighboring states, we're ready to give up before we started. The first few innings of the first game aren't going well. I play in center field and in one of the middle innings a pop fly comes my way. I dive to make the catch and roll over, popping up to throw the ball to the infield. The umpire signals "out!" and the inning is over. It is very dramatic and our team is thrilled. As we sit in the dugout our first batter gets on base. The second batter gets on base. We are "stringing some

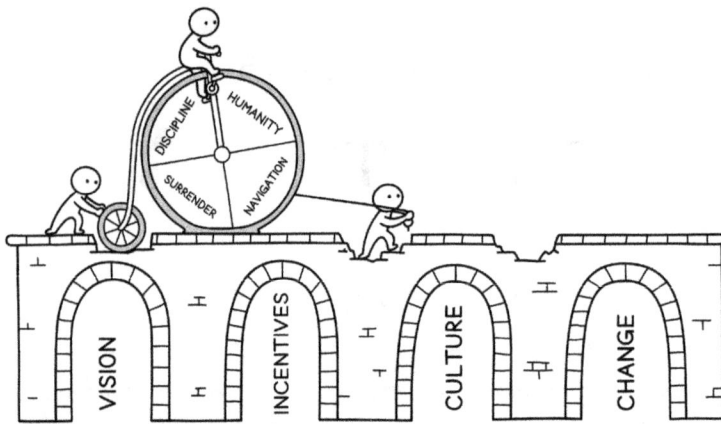

Figure 15.1 The challenges of momentum

hits together," as major leaguer Aaron Rowand would say. A comeback is underway.

The thing is, when I dove for that ball, right before the ball hit my glove, it hit the ground. My diving and rolling shielded the ump from the ball but he assumed I make the catch. As we are gaining some momentum, one of my teammates leans over and asks, "did you really make that catch?" No, I tell him, it hit the ground. Ump missed it.

Word of my non-catch spreads through the dugout like wildfire. The little bit of momentum we are generating is stopped. My admission is like a pin prick on an inflated balloon and the pop brings the team back to earth. It is like everyone who hears the catch isn't real thinks, "I knew we can't beat these guys," and things start to go bad. When one of the coaches hears the hub-bub in the dugout, he comes over, frowning, and looks me in the eye. "Why would you say that?" he says. His words are drenched in disappointment.

This event was 40 years ago, and I still think about it. At first, I thought the coach was telling me to lie, and I resented how he made me feel. With time comes perspective and after coaching kids myself I now know he was talking about momentum. He meant to say, "Why would you say that right now, when we're making a comeback? Your catch was the Inspiration for the team to start playing better, but momentum is fragile." We needed to string together some hits, keep the other team from doing the same, and maybe that little inspiration coupled with momentum could have bridged us to Continuation. My admission of the non-catch was the equivalent of the whiffle ball game to my grade school raffle sales on our momentum. It knocked us off track and we never recovered.

This story reminds me of just how fragile momentum is. It's almost ethereal in existence, like a wisp of smoke from an extinguished candle. In teaching momentum, its fragile nature often comes up, as in, "do you really think we can control something like momentum? Isn't it just easier to keep turning the lights up and down?"

They have a point. Momentum is a simple concept, but it's not easy. Let's talk about how to work on momentum.

Catch Yourself Doing Something Right

The value of being a third-party observer is noticing things you can't see when you're in the moment. As a new salesperson my manager would record my phone calls. We'd sit in the small conference room and replay the tapes. The first time I'd hear the tape I'd get distracted by my voice, "do I really sound like that?" The second time through I'd focus on what I was trying to say, like, am I close to saying what I've been taught? By the third time, I could ignore my voice, ignore my words, and focus on hearing what the prospect was saying. My performance improved by leaps and bounds when I could listen to the prospect and ignore what was in my head.

When I first started managing managers, I didn't have tape for them to review to improve their interactions with their salespeople. I'd have to recreate the "scene of the crime" so to speak by hearing what their direct reports said, comparing it to what I heard my managers say, and tie it into an action plan for improvement. The challenge for the manager was just like me listening to calls in that little conference room. They would hear my feedback and think about what they said. Hearing my feedback a third time, they could think about what their direct reports were experiencing. This is when their effectiveness would take a jump.

The most common feedback I'd give managers was about what they were focusing on when coaching their team. New managers tended to fix a negative. As in, don't do that, stop doing this, don't say that. The feedback rarely, if ever, reinforced a positive. As in, do more of that, keep doing this, say more of that. It's these latter comments that are more effective at driving behavior in sales. In some disciplines the "stop" or "change" commands may be best, but in sales, "do more" and "continue" commands make the biggest difference. My teams adopted a saying around this practice.

Catch 'em doing something right.

This focus on "keep doing what you're doing right" encourages momentum. It's a natural way to use a momentum versus motivation lens to hit your target. It makes the idea of building momentum easier to work on because it's more grounded in the day to day of work. In sales, especially after getting a no or not now answer, it's common to do a review of the calls and concentrate on what you could have done different. It's unnatural, at first, to make a list of things we're doing right that we need to continue to do.

The work of sales is made up of multiple steps and processes. Making a sale is what we can call a "complex result" made up of a lot of little pieces. Like Figure 15.2 shows.

As we review our calls and progress, it's easy to ignore all the things we are already doing and only see areas for improvement. When it comes to Sales Momentum, this is the opposite of what we need to do. For momentum to build, we need to press on our strengths more than we fix our shortcomings.

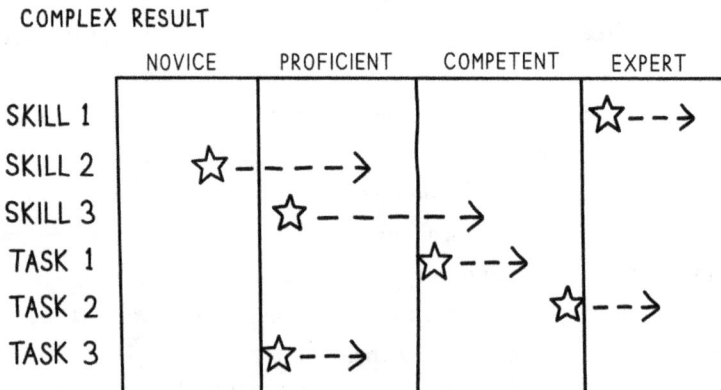

COMPLEX RESULT

	NOVICE	PROFICIENT	COMPETENT	EXPERT
SKILL 1				☆--→
SKILL 2	☆ ----→			
SKILL 3		☆ ---- →		
TASK 1			☆--→	
TASK 2				☆--→
TASK 3		☆--→		

Figure 15.2 The many pieces of complex results

For example, one of the first sales trainings I ever went to asked us on day one, "Gentlemen, is it better to be good, or is it better to be there?" This encouraged a little conversation and a little debate before our group settled on, both. We want to be there, but we also want to be good. If we were pushed to decide on one over the other, we'd want to be good. We want to be Blake or Don. We want to be really, really good. The way to help our prospects make great decisions is for us to have superior knowledge and razor-sharp questioning skills. It doesn't help to be "there" if you can't do the job, we thought.

The trainer had another take. He said,

Yes, you want to be both good and there, but it's always better to be there. More sales are made because someone is in the right place at the right time than being the best trained person in the world. Especially if you're not in front of the prospect when they are ready to buy. It's better to be "there."

He was talking about action. It's better to take action than to wait. Momentum is action. When we look through a momentum lens we recognize this right away. In the graphic, I'm saying "being there" is Skill #1. If you were in the game, you had a shot. Before your analysis of what went wrong with a sale, momentum forces you to admit that what you did best was "get there." Without that action, nothing happens. Action takes you from Inspiration to Continuation. This is what a momentum lens does for us as salespeople. It reminds us to keep moving and when we aren't moving, It forces us to find out why.

Is it something inside me? Is it my health or wealth? Is it an emotional or intellectual issue? Is it my support system or humility? Do I have someone to help mentor me through this? Is it something outside me? Do I understand and am I bought into my company's vision? Is the "juice worth the squeezing" in my incentives? Am I surrounded by a culture of excellence? Is my company helping me deal with changes in the market?

These little questions are all in service to action, dealing with the things holding us back from doing what we know we should be doing.

We should be in front of prospects. Being "there."

What To Do Now: Soak In It a While

Running errands this weekend, I drive by a giant billboard advertising Mega Millions and Powerball lottery prizes. The prize amounts are in the hundreds of millions and some lucky soul is going to win. When the prize was something like $2 billion in late 2022, a winning ticket was sold somewhere in California. That person is going to take home nearly $1 billion in cash after taxes. I read an article about it and they interviewed a wealth manager who works with lottery winners. They asked him about the best strategies for a newly minted billionaire, and his top suggestion was to make no major purchases for a year. This advisor said it's best to spend your first year getting used to the idea of never needing to think about money again. Your brain has been trained to think of the future in one way, so give it time to rewrite the story, this time with a bank account that makes millions of dollars a month in interest.

Thinking about sales and selling through a momentum lens is the same. It takes a while for your brain to get used to approaching friction and obstacles from a momentum perspective, instead of something to be motivated around. Momentum can take care of obstacles and remove friction. We all know the old saying, "a rolling stone gathers no moss," and now, with our new lenses, when we say it we mean we're focusing on what we need to do to stay in motion, what we need to do to keep the streak going.

Respect the streak.

Soak in *the Sales Momentum Mindset* for a while before making changes. Magic will happen.

Final Thought

After working with thousands of salespeople and hundreds of managers, I'm not fooling myself into thinking the switch to a Sales Momentum Mindset is going to overtake short-term Motivation. That said, there's now one fewer obstacle to deal with as I spread the word.

This book.

We've taken a step toward a common underlying proficiency (CUP), we now have a language to use. From here we can troubleshoot our momentum lens and make it easier to use. As you put some of these ideas, techniques, and tactics to work in your sales job, keep me informed, greg@chamberspivot.com. I'll be taking action, one step at a time, from my home base here in the middle of the United States, trying to string together some hits!

I wish for Fortuna to be in your favor and remember the words of Roman poet Virgil, "Audentis Fortuna iuvat"—Fortune favors the bold!

Greg Chambers—January 2023

References

Bryan, M.L., A.M. Bryce, and J. Roberts. April 2022. "Dysfunctional Presenteeism: Effects of Physical and Mental Health on Work Performance." *The Manchester School.* https://doi.org/10.1111/manc.12402.

Cave, N. August 14, 2019. "Nick Cave—The Red Hand Files—Issue #55—Do You Believe in Signs?" *The Red Hand Files.* www.theredhandfiles.com/do-you-believe-in-signs/.

Cespedes, F. and L. Yuchun. June 12, 2017. "Your Sales Training Is Probably Lackluster. Here's How to Fix It." *Harvard Business Review.*

Chambers, G.S. 2018. *The Human Being's Guide to Business Growth: A Simple Process for Unleashing the Power of Your People for Growth.* New York, NY: BEP.

Chung, D. July 20, 2017. "How to Really Motivate Salespeople." *Harvard Business Review.* https://hbr.org/2015/04/how-to-really-motivate-salespeople.

Côté, S., A. Gyurak, and R.W. Levenson. 2010. "The Ability to Regulate Emotion Is Associated With Greater Well-Being, Income, and Socioeconomic Status." *Emotion* 10, no. 6, pp. 923–933. https://doi.org/10.1037/a0021156.

Csikszentmihalyi, M. 1990. *Flow: The Psychology of Optimal Experience.* New York, NY: Harper and Row.

David, G. February 17, 2018. "The WeWork Manifesto: First, Office Space. Next, the World." *The New York Times.* www.nytimes.com/2018/02/17/business/the-wework-manifesto-first-office-space-next-the-world.html.

Dweck, C.S. 2016. *Mindset.* New York, NY: Ballantine Books Trade Paperback.

Foley, J., dir. and D. Mamet, screenplay. 1992. *Glengarry Glen Ross.*

Iso-Ahola, S.E. and C.O. Dotson. August 2016. "Psychological Momentum—a Key to Continued Success." *Frontiers in Psychology* 7. https://doi.org/10.3389/fpsyg.2016.01328.

Kahneman, D. 2011. *Thinking, Fast and Slow.* New York, NY: Farrar, Straus and Giroux.

Kepner, C.H. and B.B. Tregoe. 1965. *The Rational Manager: A Systematic Approach to Problem Solving and Decision Making.* New York, NY: McGraw-Hill.

Levitt, S.D. and J.A. List. May 28, 2009. *Was There Really a Hawthorne Effect at the Hawthorne Plant? An Analysis of the Original Illumination Experiments.* www.nber.org. www.nber.org/papers/w15016.

Lewis, M. n.d. "Against the Rules Podcast." *Season Three, Episode 1: Six Levels Down.*

Liu, L., W. Yang, R. Sinatra, C.L. Giles, C. Song, and D. Wang. 2018. "Hot Streaks in Artistic, Cultural, and Scientific Careers." *Nature* 559, no. 7714, pp. 396–399.

Lobdell, N. February 8, 2022. "Employers Should Expect Productivity Loss Monday After 2022 Super Bowl." *Challenger, Gray & Christmas, Inc.* www .challengergray.com/blog/employers-should-expect-productivity-loss-monday-after-2022-super-bowl/.

Maister, D. 2008. *Strategy and the Fat Smoker: Doing What's Obvious But Not Easy.* Boston, MA: The Spangle Press.

Mattern, W. 2023. "Review of Momentum in M & D Information Systems Sales Training." *Interview by Gregory Chambers.*

Mayo, E. and F.J. Roethlisberger. July 1, 2008. "A Field Is Born." *Harvard Business Review.* https://hbr.org/2008/07/a-field-is-born.

McGregor, I., A. Tran, E. Auger, E. Britton, J. Hayes, A. Elnakouri, E. Eftekhari, K. Sharpinskyi, O.A. Arbiv, and K. Nash. September 2022. "Higher Power Dynamics: How Meaning Search and Self-Transcendence Inspire Approach Motivation and Magnanimity." *Journal of Experimental Social Psychology* 102, p. 104350. https://doi.org/10.1016/j.jesp.2022.104350.

Nutt, A.E. February 2015. "The Science Behind Brian Williams's Mortifying Memory Flub." *The Washington Post.*

Parrish, S. n.d. *Momentum Creates Motivation.* Farnam Street. https://fs.blog/brain-food/january-8-2023/ (accessed March 4, 2023).

Payne, R.K. 2019. *A Framework for Understanding Poverty: A Cognitive Approach for Educators, Policymakers, Employers, and Service Providers.* Highlands, TX: Aha! Process, Inc.

Ram, S.K., S. Nandan, and D. Sornette. 2020. "Significant Hot Hand Effect in International Cricket." *SSRN* 3644211.

Raz, G. n.d. *Instagram: Kevin Systrom & Mike Krieger: How I Built This With Guy Raz.* NPR.org. www.npr.org/2018/01/02/562887933/instagram-kevin-systrom-mike-krieger.

Ruel, C. n.d. "Wimbledon Set for Coronavirus Windfall in Huge Pay-Out From Pandemic Insurance." *Insurance Times.* www.insurancetimes.co.uk/news/wimbledon-set-for-coronavirus-windfall-in-huge-pay-out-from-pandemic-insurance/1433146.article.

Ryu, S. and L. Fan. 2023. "The Relationship Between Financial Worries and Psychological Distress Among U.S. Adults." *Journal of Family and Economic Issues* 44, no. 1, pp. 16–33.

Thaler, R.H. and C.R. Sunstein. 2009. *Nudge: Improving Decisions About Health, Wealth, and Happiness.* New York, NY: Penguin Books.

Thomas, P.A., H. Liu, and D. Umberson. 2017. "Family Relationships and Well-Being." *Innovation in Aging* 1, no. 3, pp. 1–11. https://doi.org/10.1093/geroni/igx025.

Tversky, B. 2019. *Mind in Motion: How Action Shapes Thought.* Basic Books.

Vitale, T., C. Woloshin, and A. Bourdain. 2012. *Review of the Layover: Paris.*

Voss, C. 2017. *Never Split the Difference: Negotiating as If Your Life Depended on It.* London: Random House Business Books.

Walker, M.P. 2021. "Sleep Essentialism." *Brain* 144, no. 3, pp. 697–699. https://doi.org/10.1093/brain/awab026.

Wallace, E. March 30, 2021. "To Maximize Growth, Get Sales and Finance in Sync." *Harvard Business Review.* https://hbr.org/2021/03/to-maximize-growth-get-sales-and-finance-in-sync.

Weiner, M. 2007. *Mad Men.* Season 1, Episode 13, eds. M. Weiner and R. Veith.

Weiss, A. 1994. *Best-Laid Plans: Turning Strategy Into Action Throughout Your Organization.* Las Brisas Research Press.

About the Author

Greg Chambers is the founder of the sales-and-marketing consultancy, Chambers Pivot Industries. Companies hire Greg to create sales-and-marketing practices their people get excited about because they are a perfect fit for their cultures.

Since 2012 Greg has worked with clients in a dozen industries, including professional services, finance, and health care. He coaches clients on sales, sales management, lead generation, and database marketing.

Before opening his firm, Greg had a successful career in sales and sales management, leading to his experiences as a serial entrepreneur. He founded the cult apparel company, Mad Gringo, and cofounded the lead generation company, GoLeads.

Greg's books include, "*The Human Being's Guide to Business Growth: A simple 3 step process for unleashing the power of your people for growth*" (BEP), and the "*Amalgamate: A Mix of Ideas for Your Business*" series of booklets. Greg also wrote a novel. His thriller, "*The Legend of Mad Gringo*," follows a Hawaiian shirt-wearing protagonist who quits his corporate job and is forced to do battle with "The System."

Greg lives in Omaha with his wife, Wilson the ABC, and the Notorious Bianca B.

Index

OTHER TITLES IN THE SELLING AND SALES FORCE MANAGEMENT COLLECTION

Naresh Malhotra, Georgia Tech, Editor

- *Sales Is a Team Sport* by John Fuggles
- *Direct Selling* by Victoria Crittenden, William Crittenden, Sara Cochran, Anne Coughlan and Linda Ferrell
- *Rain Maker Pro* by Clifton Warren
- *How to be a Better Deal-Closer* by Simon P. Haigh
- *Entrepreneurial Selling* by Vincent Onyemah and Martha Rivera Pesquera
- *Selling: The New Norm* by Drew Stevens
- *A Guide to Sales Management* by Massimo Parravicini
- *Key Account Management* by Joel Le Bon and Carl Herman
- *Creating Effective Sales and Marketing Relationships* by Kenneth Le Meunier-FitzHugh and Leslie Caroline Le Meunier-FitzHugh
- *Improving Sales and Marketing Collaboration* by Avinash Malshe and Wim Biemans
- *Lean Applications in Sales* by Jaideep Motwani and Rob Ptacek
- *Competitive Intelligence and the Sales Force* by Joel Le Bon

Concise and Applied Business Books

The Collection listed above is one of 30 business subject collections that Business Expert Press has grown to make BEP a premiere publisher of print and digital books. Our concise and applied books are for...

- Professionals and Practitioners
- Faculty who adopt our books for courses
- Librarians who know that BEP's Digital Libraries are a unique way to offer students ebooks to download, not restricted with any digital rights management
- Executive Training Course Leaders
- Business Seminar Organizers

Business Expert Press books are for anyone who needs to dig deeper on business ideas, goals, and solutions to everyday problems. Whether one print book, one ebook, or buying a digital library of 110 ebooks, we remain the affordable and smart way to be business smart. For more information, please visit www.businessexpertpress.com, or contact sales@businessexpertpress.com.

www.ingramcontent.com/pod-product-compliance
Lightning Source LLC
Chambersburg PA
CBHW061304220326
41599CB00026B/4731